Heart & Soul

Heart & Soul

Living the Joy, Truth and Beauty of Your Intimate Relationship

Daphne Rose Kingma

Conari Press
Berkeley, California

Printed in the United States of America on recycled paper
Conari Press books are distributed by Publishers Group West

ISBN: 1-57324-001-X

Cover design by Floyd Carter and Christine Leonard Raquepaw

Library of Congress Cataloging-in-Publication Data

Kingma, Daphne Rose.
    Heart & Soul : living the joy, truth, and beauty of your intimate relationship / Daphne Rose Kingma.
        p.   cm.
    ISBN 1-57324-001-X : $9.95
    1. Intimacy (Psychology). 2. Interpersonal relations. I. Title. II. Title: Heart and soul.
BF575.I5K56   1995
158'.2—dc20   94-48648
                                                                                CIP

This book was floated up on sweet wings of love. My deep thanks to Sunta Oannes and Sunshine Espirit for providing the cradle in which so many of these words were written, to Tom and Eileen for my garret in Nantucket, to my blessed sister, Chris, for first bringing these words to the page, and to my dear ones at Conari Press: my editor, Mary Jane Ryan, for patience, humor, and steadfastness in love; to Karen "Grace" Bouris, for aesthetic wisdom and genteel persistence; to Emily Miles for sensitivity and graciousness; to Jennifer for laughter; to Claudia, for kindness; to David for tenacity; and to Will Glennon, for real listening.

With great love
for
Harold Yvan Le Brock
whose loving heart and exquisite soul
are joy, truth, and beauty embodied

The food of the heart is love;
the true condition of the soul is union.

CONTENTS

THE TRUTH IN LOVE

THE BEAUTY OF LOVE

Heart and Soul

We remember love in our hearts,
as the thing which, in life, made our hearts glad;
we long for love in our souls,
as the thing that will carry us home.

This book is a counterpart to *True Love: How to Make Your Relationship Sweeter, Deeper and More Passionate*, a little book I wrote to teach the emotional skills for choreographing the dance of an intimate relationship. In it, I addressed the psychological dimensions of love—how to make a relationship run smoothly, and how to treat yourself and your beloved well so you can receive the blessings and pleasures of a wonderful relationship. Many people have told me that they keep it on their bedside table, read it to one another, and practice its lessons, and that, as a result, their relationships have flourished, deepened, and transformed in ways that delight and challenge them, and also bring them great joy. This of course brings *me* great joy.

In the time since it was published, however, our world and what we ask of and give to our loves—our intimate, caring, committed, and compassionate emotional engagements—have expanded and deepened. We no longer need to know simply how to conduct our relationships so we can be comfortable in them; we want to know the meaning of relationship itself—why we get into relationships, what role they play in the schemes of our lives, and why, in spite of the pain they often cause us, we are ineffably, irrevocably drawn to them.

We're asking, from a much deeper level, about the meaning of relationship. Whereas in the past, we asked in behalf of our emotions, we are asking now with the longing of our spirits. We are beginning to perceive that every relationship is also a spiritual undertaking, that, more than just making us feel good or rescuing us from aloneness, an intimate relationship is the garden in which our spirits will blossom, the journey through which our souls will evolve, and that love, the energetic force that drives our relationships, is really what we're trying to connect with through them. Love, our brilliant spirits sense, is really the only thing that matters in this life.

I believe we now live in a time in which we have no choice but, in consciousness, to mature our love. In such elegant maturity, love is not an option but a necessity; romance is not a passionate pastime but a portal to the profound joy and compassion that is the soul's true destination; and conscious loving is an undertaking that recognizes both the desires of the heart and the transcendent longings of the soul as properties of love. For we love in both these dimensions. If the heart is the castle of the emotions, then the soul is the towering cathedral through whose high windows the blazing sunlight of pure love pours in.

Love of the heart is love of the emotional body, an elegant dance of connection enacted in the emotional realm. When we fall in love, we are suddenly united with our purest emotional essence. We feel radiant, happy, and ecstatic; we feel beautiful, hopeful, and blessed. We are transformed not only by the possibilities of this particular love, but also of life itself. Gladness is with us and we feel suddenly illumined, and when we live in an intimate relationship, we continue this heartful journey. Here the sharing of feelings—delight and sorrow, fear and rage, anguish and joy—connects us to one another to a very high degree.

Love of the heart is an exquisite, endlessly changing tableau, the play and interplay of emotions between two human beings. But the love of the soul is love supreme. It is love in our spiritual essence and of our eternal belonging. In this deep love we ascend above our emotions—how we feel, what's troubling us—and into the realm of mystical, nonmaterial essence, the realm of the ecstatic.

For in our souls, we are all warp and weft of the one great seamless cloth, woven together of all that we have been, all that we shall be—our victories and majesties and sorrows, our tragedies and grand heroic moments. In the soul's love we sense far within us, as if written in faint, faded ink on the ancient notebooks of our genes, that we have all been all things—both male and female, parent and child, abuser and abused, villager and king. To behold one another through this great encompassing love, love indivisible, love uncompromising, brilliant, radiant, and immense, is to behold the whole of human history, the face of God, in a single human being's eyes.

This book, then, is about the interface of our heart's needs—for passion, romance, companionship, and just plain fun—and our soul's need to be united with all that is and ever has been in a state of exquisite, seamless union.

We are now actively seeking this union. For what we have made of ourselves in this world—our objects and achievements, our clever technology, our getting and spending—has not moved us at the deepest level. We "have it all" and yet are still awash with longing. Intuitively we know that it is only love and, in human experience, relationship at the intimate personal level that can chime the deep chord which reminds us of the indelible union that is not only our birthright but our spiritual destination.

This book is about these journeys—the journey of the heart to the love that flowers in joyful emotions, and the journey of the soul's deep longing to carry us all back home. These are not two separate journeys, actually, but a single, parallel, interwoven adventure. For, we are not only personalities, psychological beings with histories and emotions, but also souls who have as their ultimate longing a reunion with the divine; and it is this union for which all our relationships are a metaphor.

As we near the end of the twentieth century, this longing for union is no longer merely a metaphor, however. It is being enacted as boundaries of every kind are giving way and breaking down, both beautifully and in ways that appall and frighten us. The message in all this upsetting, asked-for and unasked-for transformation is that the boundaries *must* break down—within ourselves (between what we're willing to look at and what we insist on denying), in our intimate relationships (between ourselves and our sweethearts, lovers, husbands, or wives), and in relation to our spiritual essence and its true destination.

Love is the one experience of the human condition that allows us to feel unequivocally, beautifully, and deeply that our true condition is not isolation but union. In recognition of that stunning truth, I offer this book as a guide to the further journey of your love, the love of your heart and soul.

In Exaltation of Love

Since time immemorial, men and women have loved one another—desperately, madly, sweetly, with unbridled dangerous passion, with the compassion of their kind hearts, to the depth of their souls. Love knows no bounds. There is no country, province, or people to which it has ever been irrelevant, and whenever you fall in love, you join the company of lovers of all times in living out one of life's greatest themes.

What you feel when you fall in love is universal. However ordinary or simple your own love may appear to be, to your heart and soul it is a grand love. Like David and Bathsheba, Anthony and Cleopatra, Romeo and Juliet, Abelard and Heloise, your love, too, is an experience of wonder and ecstatic belonging that will draw you into life's most tragic and beautiful moments. Through love you become part of a sacred tradition, that great lineage of all those who have plighted their troth, promised their hearts to one another, chosen to live and die for love, and known that love was the only thing worth living for.

We need love.

We seek love because in every cell of our being we know that love is the only thing we cannot without 'n each breath, with each beat of our hearts, we know this. This is why no matter what else we may do or pursue in our lives, love is always our highest goal, our farthest reach, our most passionate quest.

That is because in our hearts we know that in this world of sorrow and betrayal, love is what we have to hold on to. Only love can make our hearts sing in even the deepest of darkness, can let our souls come to peace in the midst of even the most tremendous travail. Love is the only thing we will take with us when we walk out of this life.

Everything that we are—personality, body, emotions, achievements, reputation, bank accounts, friendships, trophies, Academy Awards, gold medals, houses, furniture, parents and children, memories even, and great expectations—will all pass away. Only love, the beautiful light, will remain. For love is the light that calls us into being and awaits us when we have stepped our last curtsy across life's stage. Love is the mystical, unconditionally all-affirming Yes. Love is *being* itself, consciousness itself, the energy which itself is the substance and essence of life.

We love in the midst of Love.

The love we feel, the love we need, the love we give is surrounded by the great Love that is the matrix and cradle and blessing and essence of our being. This Love is the vessel, recipe, and map for all the words, gifts, and happenings, beautiful moments and touching exchanges which in this life we call loving, being loved, or feeling love. It is the limitless sea in which all our human experiences of love—the love of lovers and sweethearts, of husbands and wives, of parents for their children, brothers and sisters for one another, of dearest friends and compassionate strangers—swim like the vast and variegated multitude of fish in the infinite ocean.

Love as we know it and live it—the love of duty, as a man to his country; of pleasure, as in the flower of friendship; of passion and ecstasy, as in romance; of commitment, as in all the changing vicissitudes of our intimate relationships—all these are faces, miniature and particular embodiments, of the faceless, infinitely graceful, endlessly tenderhearted Love that is the medium in which we all live and breathe.

All the love that we know and need and seek and make is but the corner of a postcard from this infinite and beautiful landscape. When, through a particular moment of love in our own lives we feel suddenly exalted, we discover our omnipresent connection to that great, that infinite Love; and when, through the willingness to throw our hearts *wide* open, we suddenly apprehend that we ourselves are a reflection of and participants in that one great Love, then our human relationships become radiant and illumined, the sacred chalice from which we sip of the Love that is truly divine.

The Joy of Love

Happiness is the joy of the heart;
joy is the happiness of the soul

Appreciate the Moment

This moment, this day, this relationship, and this life are all exquisite, unique, and unrepeatable. There will be no moment exactly like this one (the yellow light spilling in through the thin white louvers on the window, the sound of the men at work in the street and, in the living room, of the pages of the newspaper turning). There will be no day that repeats precisely the sweet events of this day (the waking and sleeping, the beautiful dreams before waking, the precious and even the ordinary conversations, the clothes you have chosen to wear, and the way that today you are wearing them; the way the wind is today, clattering the shutters, scattering the leaves, the thoughts—all sixty thousand of them—that have passed like bright kites through your mind).

There will be no love, no dearly beloved, exactly like this one (the man who pronounces your name in just such a way, with his beautiful voice; the man who brings flowers, whose words move your heart so tremblingly softly, whose arms hold you this way and that way, embracing, consoling, protecting; the woman whose fragrance enchants you, whose head on your chest when you sleep is the sweet weight of bliss, whose kisses are blessings, whose laughter is sunlight, whose smile is pure grace).

There will be no lifetime exactly like this one, no other, not ever again, not this birth, not this particular story, this mother and father, these houses and walls, these strangers and friends—*and how we moved through it all, with such beauty, touching each other, dancingly stepping, curtsying, bowing across all the stages, filling the rooms of our lives with this joy, this sweet love. . . .*

There will be no other way to live this life, only the way you have chosen to live it, only the way that, moment by moment, you fill up its houses and cradles and baskets, its cupboards and drawers—with which beautiful things, what small scraps and treasures—and only the way that you fill up your heart—with what feelings, which lovely emotions—*and the memory of her standing there, in the light, by the window, her blonde hair in sunlight . . . and the image of him standing there and saying, "always, forever, till death do us part"*—and your mind—with what words, which endlessly coddled concerns, what difficult puzzles and brilliant solutions, what emptiness . . . waiting for God.

This moment, this day, this relationship, this life are all unique, exquisite, unrepeatable. Live every moment as if you, indelibly, knew this.

Aspire to a Spiritual Relationship

To have a spiritual relationship is to consciously acknowledge that above all we are spiritual beings and that the process of our spiritual refinement is our true undertaking in this life. When you have a spiritual relationship, you choose to embody this truth in love. You shift context and focus. Whereas an emotional relationship has as its focus the contents of the relationship itself, a spiritual relationship sees the spirit's well-being and the soul's journey as its overriding undertaking. Whereas the romantic relationship operates in time, the spiritual union has timeless infinity as its context. Rather than framing itself in life, on earth, it knows that we are all far more than we appear to be and it joyfully claims as its territory a cosmos that radiates and scintillates, that includes an infinity of angels, and all the stunning coincidental events that are the mysterious instruments of God.

When you love one another in spirit, along with loving, desiring, cherishing, adoring, and protecting your beloved, you will also be the champion of your beloved's spiritual well-being, ensuring that she will make the choices that will allow for her soul's evolution. This may mean creating a quiet environment in which your spirits can flourish, or doing those things—meditating, praying, throwing away the television set—that will encourage a reunion of your souls.

To have an intimate relationship that is also spiritual defies our Western ordinary thinking, for in a spiritual relationship we are not seeking the satisfactions of the ego in a conventional way. Instead, we are aware that we are spirits and that we are on the spirit's journey.

The spiritual relationship is gracious, easy, considerate, and kind. Because it has stepped off the merry-go-round of ego concerns, it can be generous and patient, can behold the beloved not just as a person doing this or that, but as a soul on a journey. For, to the spiritually beloved there is always a sense of this greater focus. Because of it, each action and experience takes on a different coloration. The disappointments of the moment and even the tragedies of a lifetime are seen not as happenings which are absolutes in themselves but finite, irritating specks on the larger screen of vision.

A great spiritual love does not exclude the psychological and physical—in any spiritual relationship the partners will always support each other in these realms with healing and attention—but when you love one another in the spirit, your love will also be a reminder of the infinite context, the true destination. Remembering this will give your love an exalted, crystalline, and truly luminous quality. For if your emotional relationship is a jewel, then your spiritual relationship is the light that shines through it.

REJOICE TOGETHER

When we think of being with one another emotionally, we ordinarily think of empathizing with one another in times of pain or misery. While it's certainly true that in our sufferings we have a great need for empathy, we also need positive empathy—rejoicing—a delighted feeling with, for all our joys.

Rejoicing is feeling joy, allowing the feelings of exhilaration and delight to enter your being and fill you with a fine, ecstatic sense of celebration. We all need to rejoice, to slather ourselves with exultation, because life is hard, and at times our paths are very difficult. We need to rejoice because joy is our true state of being, and when we rejoice we return to it for a moment. We need to rejoice because there isn't enough rejoicing in the world. And we need to rejoice together because in this world of self-involvement and nonstop competition, it's often hard to find a kindred soul with whom to rejoice.

Rejoicing is empathy at the encouraging end of the spectrum, and although you may think it's easier to rejoice than to commiserate with someone, rejoicing, too, can be difficult. As a matter of fact, a lot of people feel so defeated in their own lives that instead of being able to celebrate with anyone else, they feel jealousy or self-pity. Indeed, unless you've really been able to feel your own joy, you may have a difficult time rejoicing, even with your beloved.

So in order to rejoice together—to double your joy, to share your beloved's pleasures, and truly celebrate them—allow yourself to rejoice first of all in your own life, about all the things that delight you, that brighten your day, that make your heart glad. Celebrate your victories, exult in your own achievements. Then you'll be well prepared to really rejoice with your sweetheart.

Rejoicing together is breathing in joy, being together at the moment of beauty (of soul-washing tears, of life-changing praise), in the hour of unbridled happiness, of sweet—or stunning—success. It is to be the loving witness at the epiphany of a talent (his book; her photography exhibit; his all-star game; her tennis match), to celebrate special occasions: birthdays, anniversaries, life achievement awards. It is also to rejoice in all the cycles of your love—times and years you have shared, crises you have lived through, reunions that rekindled your love, and even all the good fights and their healing resolutions.

We must rejoice together because rejoicing begets itself. It brings us more joy, more hilarity, a greater sense that life is radiance, splendor, pleasure, and fun. So one by one and, above all, together, rejoice!

OPEN TO THE ECSTATIC ENERGY

Life is breath, movement. So long as you are capable of movement, you inhabit life and the energy of life inhabits you. In this state, every step you take, every word you utter, every thought that passes through the electronic magic circuitry of your brain, and every single gesture you enact is an expression of your vivid aliveness, a sign that you are a mortal, alive human being.

In relationships, we join these energies with one another through passion and affection. Sexuality and sensuality are the media of our passionate connection, the arena where flesh and spirit meet; and affection is the medium through which we express our fond, caring love.

Sometimes in our overemphasis on verbal communication, we forget that we are also bodies and that as physical beings, too, we have a unique and powerful language. In our bodies, we "feel" and know things often before we can even begin to articulate them. Through our bodies, we share our love in an immediate, instinctual way that conveys a depth of feeling beyond words.

The language of the body is this energy, the invisible ecstatic pulse which is the essence of life itself. We often think of our aliveness only as form—the bodies we inhabit—and not as the force of life, or energy, that flows through them. In so doing, we miss the opportunity to feel our own aliveness, and, in relationship, to be nourished by that mysterious spiritual commodity that is another person's "energy." Yet it is precisely the "energy"—of a city, a person, a particular piece of music or an emotional exchange—that actually moves us at the deepest level. Nothing reveals this more clearly than a body which, through illness, is being drained of its energetic essence, and no one demonstrates the existence of this energy more beautifully than children.

In our intimate relationships, when we shift our attention from the material form—what we look like, what we're wearing, how in or out of shape we are—and move it into the energetic realm, we enter the grand, new, mystical arena in which we experience love itself as an expression of this energy. Instead of feeling it only as an emotion, we sense it also as a mystic invisible pulse, the heart-filling throb, the luminous shivers that tell our bodies we have truly "felt" our love.

To move your consciousness from the awareness of substance to energy, and to seek the persons whose energy, for you, is ecstatic, is to immediately expand your repertoire of love. When you do, you will not only be able to talk about the love you feel, you will actually be able to "feel" it as the tingling, brilliant, ecstatic life essence in your body. So open your heart—and every cell of your being—to the luminous life-changing wisdom that is your soul's ecstatic energy.

Stop Trying So Hard

 Most of us conduct our lives primarily through a combination of effort, exertion, and ambition: If I work hard, then . . . If it's very difficult, then . . . If I keep at it, then . . . If I do it better, longer, or stronger than anyone else, then . . . surely, I'll be successful, achieve my ambitions.

This inclination toward the difficult, demanding, and competitive is so much the hallmark of our culture that it has all but become a knee-jerk reaction in our personal lives as well. It is an occupation of the mind and a preoccupation of the personality; it is the antithesis of grace, of ease.

Unfortunately, the same sad predilection toward effort that we apply to work we also apply to love. We use the ghastly expression that we are "working on" our relationships, as if they were cars that needed repairs or gold mines from which with endless effort we might dredge up the sacred paydirt of a wonderful relationship.

When we look at love in this way, we degrade it. Love becomes a project instead of a miracle, and we miss the fruits of its marvelous quirkiness. We can become so involved with "working on" it, "sharing" our feelings, "trying" to communicate better, or "learning" how to negotiate, that love, the mysterious power that brought us together in the first place, is all but stifled in the process.

This isn't to say that a good relationship doesn't prosper from the appropriate forms of focused attention, but rather that if you become fixated on it in this way, you'll squeeze out all the juice and be left with nothing but an empty rind.

The truth is that most of the things we try for in life are just that—trials and trying. But when we slip, by accident, into the effortless space, we stand face-to-face with the miracle—and the lesson—that the things that move us most deeply are almost always a gift.

Love, real love, is a grace, unattainable through effort. It is a gift of the spirit, not a consequence of endeavor. It is not an outcome to be worked toward, but a treasure to be received. So when love magically, spontaneously appears, don't try; just let it in. And when your relationship whimsically, unexpectedly, grandly offers you beautiful moments, don't try to analyze or repeat them, just open your heart and allow them to burst into bloom.

CAST OFF YOUR PRIDE

Pride is a spurious, dangerous emotion that can stand in the way of deep love. It's what you feel when your truer feelings are too hard to feel—that you have been (or may be) abandoned, that you're not enough, that your looks, achievements, wealth, social status, clothes, children, houses, jobs, professions won't in some way (or in some important context that you're measuring by) measure up.

Pride is what we have, do, feel, preserve instead of all of the above. It gets us through the rough times, allows us, in difficult circumstances, in spite of our feared inadequacies, to carry on. But pride, embedded, taken on as a personality trait, is a dangerous attribute. It stands between you and what is or might be: love, a new friend, the healing of an old wound, a better job, a kiss, a miracle.

When you get too involved with your pride—the way you think you ought to be treated, how important you are, how insulted you feel because "they" overlooked you—you miss what's right in front of your eyes—this beautiful, unrepeatable moment, to say nothing of the chance to step forward exactly as yourself.

Pride in relationship creates distance. If you want to be treated like a proud, kingly lion, you can be, but you'll be all alone in the jungle. Instead of coming to your beloved in vulnerability, revealing yourself, asking for what you need and allowing her beautiful love to flow in, you'll stand like the Wizard of Oz in her presence, all puffed up with your pride, insisting she be your accomplice in shoring up your illusions.

We often use the phrase "pride and joy" to speak of who or what makes us proud, gives us joy. In that sense, pride is a heart-swelling joy. But pride as a private emotional stance is the antithesis of joy. Far from bringing you joy, it will stand in joy's way. Joy thrives on freedom; joy flows. If the place in your heart that is longing for joy is already jammed full of pride, joy, the unwelcome guest, may just slink away.

So give up your pride. It may preserve your dignity, protect you from all the judgments you fear, but, in the end, all it will do for you, really, is leave you alone . . . with your pride.

DISCOVER SEX AS SACRED REUNION

Our sexuality is one of the loveliest, most complex and satisfying aspects of our intimate relationships. It is where we gather in the flesh to be joined, connected, and bonded. It can bring us joy or disappointment. It can be the source of our most painful betrayals, or of the highest moments of our ecstatic love.

Just as bringing our bodies together in the sexual encounter reminds us that we are bodies, essentially physical beings, so orgasm, the moment of blossoming ecstasy, connects us to the spiritual essence within us. Taken in total, making love is the movement of the mystic, electric current that bears eloquent witness to the fact that we are not just physical beings but temples where the spirit resides.

To apprehend your lovemaking in this way is to move toward the sacred in your sexual relationship. It is to ask more of it, give more to it, and receive more, far more, from it than you can ever expect from the how-to-improve-your-sex-life articles in popular magazines. Although handy-dandy advice columns and erotic manuals may indeed solve some of your sexual machinery problems, they will drop you off at the doorway of sex as a gymnasium, romance novel, or power trip, leaving you with only a sensate thrill. Thus you are denied the magnificent opportunity of experiencing your sexual encounters as a spiritual reunion of the highest order.

For in making love, it is not only our bodies that are happily and deliciously engaged; but, because of the irresistible magnetism that sexual attraction is, we are also invited to contemplate in the mind and actually experience in the body that spirit lives and moves within us.

Through sex we enter the timeless, boundary-less moment. We partake of the one experience above all others in life which allows us the bliss of true union. Here ego and all its concerns are erased, and the self is dissolved in utter surrender. To know, feel, and discover this in the presence of another human being, as we are invited to do in making love, is to be brought face-to-face with one of the greatest mysteries of human existence—that we are spirit, embodied, and that as human beings, we are partaking in this miracle.

To experience your sexual relationship in this way is to elevate it to the sacred encounter it is. In so doing, you will experience your body as a vessel of the divine, your orgasm as a gift of the spirit, and your beloved as he or she with whom you are gifted to share a taste of eternal bliss.

BE EXTRAVAGANT WITH YOUR PRAISE

Everybody has hundreds of things to be praised—even a total stranger. If you stopped for a moment and looked at the person beside you on the bus, ahead of you at the check-out stand, pumping gas at the service station, you could see, sense, hear, feel something so fine, or beautiful, or true about that human being that you would realize how worthy it is of being remarked upon. And if you uttered that praise, that mini-celebration of this person's specialness, you just might see a stranger suddenly burst into bloom.

How much more, then, does your beloved, the one special being you've chosen to honor, enjoy, and cherish, merit the celebrating words of praise, admiration, and acknowledgment that will make his or her heart sing. All too often, proximity breeds, if not contempt, then blindness and amnesia. We forget to acknowledge those sterling attributes, whimsical quirks, and singular passions that caused us to fall in love in the first place. Once we've "captured" a mate (precisely because of all the attributes we so cherish and admire—her beautiful eyes, his wonderful wit, the amazing softness of her skin, his big bear rug of a chest), we often get lazy, stingy even, with the warm bath of praise that could wash away hurts and deepen our bonds of connection.

It's as if we use praise as a lure, to snag somebody to love, but then seem to forget that praise, the out-loud, out-spoken, uproarious celebration of all the things that are good, great, special, and rare about that one very fine person, is really the life's breath of love.

Praise opens the heart and refreshes the soul of the one who is praised. It sculpts and enhances the very behaviors it honors, encourages them to multiply. Praise creates change. It refashions the soul. By quietly showing forth the magnificence already there, it inspires the ongoing creation of an ever finer human being.

So if you want joy in your relationship, an enduring sense of its specialness, the feeling that you are loved by (and are loving) a most extraordinary human being, be accurate, consistent, generous, and extravagant with your praise.

ACCEPT THE GLORIOUS
COMPROMISES OF LOVE

There is a component of sacrifice to every intimate relationship, no matter how blissful or harmonious it may be. When you choose to love one person in a special, committed way, you are unchoosing—or giving up—your option to choose all others, for a time at least, in that same particular way.

Love—the feeling—and "being in love"—the ravishing experience—make us willing, even dare-devilishly eager, to make these sacrifices. It's a joy to choose one above all others, a delight to feel graced and blessed by your beloved's uniquely delicious, heartwarming presence.

But this choosing, grand as it is, and willing as we are to make it, is also symbolic of the many choices, little renunciations and revisions of priority that, for love, we shall come to make as we walk the path of relationship. There's a great deal we do (or discontinue doing) precisely and only because we love. Jane postponed graduate school to mother Paul's two children, whose mother had died of cancer. Mark moved from the house he'd built for himself to live in the town where René, his new love, was a tenured professor.

Such revisions are only the tip of the iceberg. Each day, in love, you will be faced with decisions and choices, invited to make compromises which represent a willingness to meet your beloved halfway on the playing field of love. Thus, you may find yourself adapting to uncomfortable schedules or meticulous (or sloppy) housekeeping habits (the proverbial toothpaste folded up wrong—or far too perfectly), taking vacations you never imagined (but ended up loving anyway), preparing foods you never even liked, or entering into financial arrangements that stretch your equanimity to the limit.

A compromise—what you do for love—needs to be just that: a conscious revision of your own preferences. As such, it becomes a creative, imaginative act, an opportunity to expand, to experience life in a new and surprisingly beautiful frame. But above all, it shows you the depth of your love. For when we smooth off the corners of our own dogmatic priorities, we reach toward one another. In so doing we see that love, the deep recognition of the soul of our beloved—and not all the endless particulars of life—is truly the most important thing there is.

Attend to the Unfolding

Your relationship is constantly in a state of evolution. Like the river, ever moving, you can never step into the same current twice. When you "fall in love," there are certain things that draw you to a person, hook you in, connect you, and then, as time goes on, things change. You change. He or she changes. The way you were together is changed—through aging and illness, by external events (earthquakes, drops and gains in the stock market), and internal revisions (emotional and spiritual awakenings), or by the direction that, because of personal or economic necessity, you find your mutual life taking. (He had asthma; we moved to New Mexico. She lost her job; we joined the Peace Corps.)

You may have had an idea of what you wanted your relationship to look like, the direction you hoped it would take; but life and its surprising little tricks will probably tease you off your intended path. As it does, the actual events and external circumstances you face will also become a map of what's happening to you and your beloved inside your relationship.

Paying attention to what's happening, therefore, and communicating about it, is of the utmost importance. It will keep you real. It will also keep you in conscious contact with each other—and with all the changes your partner may be going through as his or her individual life (and your mutual one) unfolds. This keeping in touch (and being aware of each other's feelings) is the stuff that intimacy is made of. If you stop paying attention (or communicating), you may lose the feeling of connectedness that lies at the heart of love.

But paying attention also has a larger purpose. Life is shaping us all the time, and we are being constantly invited to move toward the deeper layers of ourselves—and of life itself—through all the experiences that life doles out to us. In a similar way, as your relationship unfolds, it is asking you to expand. For example, you may be being asked to express yourself more—to cry, to get angry, to say the things you were afraid of saying—or to find a way to go deeper together—to join a discussion group, to meditate, to pray.

But whatever you do, life and your relationship are constantly inviting you to change. If you're not paying attention, you may miss brilliant opportunities—to make more money, to embark on a new career, to open your heart, to create a deeper sexual relationship, to expand the reach of your love.

So always notice what's happening—to yourself, to your heart, to your mutual life, and, above all, to your beloved—so you won't miss a single chance to spice up, shore up, deepen, enhance, or renew your marvelous relationship.

LIE IN THE ROSE PETALS

Wouldn't it be wonderful if you could just say, "Come lie with me in the rose petals,"—if you had the rose petals to lie in, if you had enough time to lie down, sweetly, deliciously, in them, if you had the whispering beautiful imagination to utter such words in the first place.

To be able to say such words would mean that some wonderful things had already happened to you—that your spirit is already free, that your heart is open and clear, that you have already been touched so deeply, so dearly, by someone that you could want to lie down in a bed of rose petals with him, with her (feeling the texture, breathing the fragrance, savoring the mystic effervescence), that you have arranged your life, your day, your way of being so that, in fact, you could partake of your own wise wild invitation.

To say "Come lie with me in the rose petals" would mean that you have the courage to ask, to risk, to be foolish, to hope and expect, to want, and to wildly imagine, to magically dream.

Come, lie with me in the rose petals and let us bow down to the scent of the roses, perfuming our sorrows, diminishing the grasp of all our tragedies, unravelling the grip of all the ordinary awful tasks that bind us, dull us, and so tediously unshine us. Let us slip for a moment into the sweet bliss of roses, into a breathless breathtakingly lovely bevy of kisses, of magic, of always . . .

How long has it been since you've spoken such courtly, majestic, and fanciful words?

There is no time like this moment. There are no words more special than the ones you feel moved to utter, no risk more worthy than the one you fancy taking, to move you farther, more deeply, into the sweet bliss of love.

Therefore, take courage; be a jester and a hero; and say to your darling beloved (while the sun watches, while the moon hovers, while the birds sing): "Come lie with me in the rose petals, and let us rejoice in our love."

PRACTICE HAPPINESS TO PREPARE FOR JOY

Happiness is a state of well-being and delight, of felicity, beatitude, and comfort. Happiness is a lightness of the heart. It is the reward of play, the antithesis of worry, the medicine for despair. We experience it in moments as a delicious, shivering rush and long for it always as the place we'd like to inhabit. We feel happy when we fall in love; we want to be happy when we marry or live with our beloved; we hope to live happily ever after. Happiness is the blissful measure of how well we're doing in our lives.

Happiness is a goal of the heart, of the temporal, personal self. It enhances the feel of our lives. We're more at ease when we're happy, more generous and kind. Happiness begets happiness. When we're happy, we like to share our delicious happiness.

Because happiness is an emotional state, it is contingent upon behavior and experience: *she made me happy; he didn't make me happy. I was happy then; I'm not happy now.* It's the up on the emotional seesaw, but it confines us in the emotional realm.

Joy, on the other hand, is a spiritual state of being, the condition of ultimate ease and grace, a swim in the sweet, eternal all-rightness of things. It's the state we're in when the things of life, even what makes us happy or unhappy, are no longer of any concern. Joy is a spiritual condition, the eloquent state of perfection of which happiness, on the emotional level, is the microcosmic prototype.

We can't always feel pure joy; most of our lives aren't arranged so we can just sit around and drink of deep bliss. But we can, as we live out our lives, prepare for joy by practicing happiness; for happiness, unlike joy, is something we can consciously create. Happiness is created through kindness, through the experience of beauty, through generous deeds and surprises, through fun and the careful, responsible use of all of our personal resources. Happiness abounds when we share it: when you pass along a compliment, when you savor an achievement with a friend, when you praise your children's homework, when you admire your wife's new haircut or enjoy a great movie with your husband.

So be happy. For happiness, the feeling of delight, of sheer unmitigated pleasure at the marvelous rightness of things, is the prelude, preface, and practice of the joy that is absolute bliss.

PLAY

It's no big secret that we all need recreation, relaxation, diversion, distraction, surcease even, from the deadly dailiness of life. There's even a section every Sunday in the newspaper to lure, cajole, and entice us into the travels and leisures that represent a categorical departure from the mundane because we all need diversion so much.

But real play is more than simply stopping the doing of what you do too much of. It's a ridiculous, imaginative, creative approach, a new way of looking at life and entering into it magically—upside down, sideways, or backwards. It's the rabbit in the hat of your usual Saturday night.

When we were children we knew how to play. Play came easily, almost without thinking. It was a gift, a sort of spiritual inheritance. We understood then that doing nothing or making up something to do—anything—out of the whole bright cloth of our rich imaginations would nourish and restore our spirits. So a mudpie was a birthday cake, a stick a sword, and green crepe paper a deadly dragon.

But now we don't know how to play. Not like that. So much of what as adults we call play is really very passive. We want to be spoon-fed, done to, and entertained—perhaps because every day we put so much energy into so many things we don't really believe in that it's almost as if, without making an effort, we want to be repaid. We have an inner sadness, anger even, that our imaginations, our creativity, and above all, our time, are not being spent on the things that just in themselves would brighten our spirits.

Real play, play of the spirit, is not about filling the void, but delving into it. It springs from the heart; it will nourish you in the deep places. Indeed the play of the soul is a very high form of play. It asks that more than merely amusing yourself, you reach in for the avocations and relaxations that speak to your spirit's deep needs—for joy, for freedom, for humor, for beauty. And it's active, not passive. Rather than quietly amusing you it requires that you stand up and change your life patterns: by giving an hour a day to quiet contemplation, by selling your car and buying a hot air balloon, by taking an early retirement and becoming the Amerigo Vespucci of your own life. It means stepping out onto your own frontiers, beyond the familiar, beyond the known, beyond what the world can deliver to you and into the No-Man's Land of your own imagination.

In this high play, surely, we shall become once again like children. For the true play of the spirit is discovery and trust, the happy conviction that, through our own imaginations, we will be perfectly led to the play that deeply delights us.

Honor the Anger Inside You

Believe it or not, anger is one of the richest components of your emotional makeup. It is the feeling above all others by which you declare your rights to the world. When you express it appropriately, you give notice, as it were, to the people whose behavior offends you. You say, in effect, I won't tolerate your mistreatment of me; there will be consequences—my anger—for your conduct.

Anger is a self-honoring emotion. It's your way of saying you value yourself as a person, you believe you deserve to be treated well, and you're willing to growl, scratch, and bite (figuratively speaking, of course) to make your point if the treatment you deserve isn't readily forthcoming.

There are two kinds of anger: existential anger and emotional anger. Existential anger—anger about "the way things are" (your club foot, the unbearable loss when your wife was killed in a plane crash)—is the soul's disappointment about the human condition. As persons, we can only feel this anger and accept it. But when it comes to anger in the emotional realm (the way your sweetheart snapped when he was driving you to the airport) handling anger is a dance of reclaiming your self-esteem and power. To deal with this second kind of anger, your anger in relationship, here are a few important tips:

○ It's better let out than kept in.

○ It can be a mad dog, so when you do let it out, use a muzzle.

○ Try to be exact. What *exactly* is it you're angry about?—not "everything," but "the way you snapped at me on the way to the airport."

○ Remember that the purpose is to heal—yourself (by finally releasing your anger instead of holding it as a knot inside you), your beloved (by giving him a chance to change his behavior or ask for your forgiveness), and your relationship (by clearing the slate for something new to occur).

Expressing your anger can make you feel good emotionally because you get that weight off your chest. But what does it do for your soul? It clears the path for your soul's deeper work.

Share Your Transcendent Moments

 At one time or another most of us will have what is sometimes called a "spiritual experience." One day, without trying or imagining, we will slip through the sieve of life as we ordinarily know it and into the experience of some mysterious happening. It may be a beautiful light, a feeling of infinite bliss, a coincidence so profoundly stunning as to convince us, absolutely, if only for a moment, that we are part of a world and a system of being so immense, so elegant, and so rarified in its extraordinary design that we bow before it, are awed and forever changed.

In the past we conceived of such things as happening only to mystics and saints, people whose whole lives were clearly set out on the spiritual path. But the truth is that what we refer to as a "spiritual experience"—a direct encounter with the mystery we inhabit and of which we are each a flawless part—is an event for which our whole lives are a metaphor and toward which our whole lives are leading.

Just as emotions are a natural expression of the personality, experience of the numinous—the sacred and exalted in our midst—is the organic experience of the soul. In fact, if you carefully ask each person you know, you will be surprised to discover how many people have had an encounter with the sacred.

When you are gifted with such an experience, a moment of touching transcendence, and when you share it with your beloved, you have, as it were, invited him or her to partake of the secrets of your soul. "As I lay on my bed, I felt a benign and beautiful presence enter the room. I thought perhaps it was death, but it was gentle, luminous, and kind. It stood beside me for a small, short while, granting me an unspeakable sweet experience of bliss, and then it was gone."

"I lay on the grass, staring mindlessly up at the clouds, when suddenly they parted and opened, revealing into my vision an ineffable, endless, radiant presence of light. I was bathed in the light; it subsumed me and carried me up, so that I wasn't myself anymore, but one with it, with the light."

Such breathtaking, sacred experiences are benedictions of the divine. Although we hear of them as isolated, extraordinary, or even "paranormal" events, none of us stands outside of their reach; for they are the true inheritance of our souls, and the more we are softly open to them, the more they will occur.

So share with your beloved your experience of the sacred. By so doing you will be reminded that the divine is always with us. We live in the midst of it; and it lives in the midst of us.

Rest in the Radiance of Forgiveness

The very exquisite proximity of love and the vulnerability we bring to it guarantee that not only will we create pain for those we love, but also get hurt ourselves. It's in the cards; it's in the stars. The other side of the joy of love is the hurt it often delivers us to.

While love inevitably wounds us, the medicine for the wounds of love—the pain we dole out and the excruciating blows we receive—is both simple and almost impossible: forgiveness. In the eye-for-an-eye modality, we all deserve revenge; there isn't a good reason to forgive anybody for anything. But forgiveness isn't a psychological act—making him suffer so you can feel cheaply better about yourself; it's an operation of the soul on behalf of the wounded heart.

We all have unforgivable, horrible things we have to forgive. If they weren't unforgivable—worthy of blind revenge—we wouldn't need to learn how to forgive. But we must. And we do. And we can.

Forgiveness isn't forgetting (suppressing), overlooking (playing dumb), or pretending (with rafts of rationalizations), that the horrible thing didn't happen. It is, quite to the contrary, wholly taking it in, feeling the dimensions of the wound, and then, through the soul's alchemistry, inviting it to change.

How do you forgive? First, put yourself in your abuser's place: If you were he, in those—or any—circumstances, might you, could you possibly ever have done the same thing? Second, take the person out of the context in which she's wounded you and put her for a moment into some other context—where she was, for example, when she was a child with her parents, or where he was an hour, a day or a week before he did the thing that hurt you. Then open your eyes and your heart and let your compassion flow in.

Forgiveness is twice blessed. It frees the one forgiven from guilt, and you from bitterness. Forgiveness sheds light on the subject. It lets love, instead of judgment, shine in. Judgment curdles the soul; forgiveness invites your spirit to burst into bloom.

BE AVAILABLE TO THE MYSTERY

Love of the heart and soul is mysterious. It takes chances. It believes in miracles. It is breath, movement, magic, music, the evanescent moment, the blissful surprise. To be available to the mystery means that you are open, expectant, waiting—continually poised on tiptoe, prepared to be illumined—not locked in your own expectations of how you think it should happen.

In life and in love, this means living free, with your mind set loose from its gears, not endlessly chattering inside, "but it has to be this way," or "I thought it was going to be that way." Our own ideas, those tidy little constructions of the intellect and psyche, just serve to limit our reality, shut down the possibilities, create a universe only as complex and rarified as the busy minds that invent it. Indeed, if we're too invested in the concepts of the mind, we will only recognize the things and allow into our lives the kinds of experiences that confirm what our minds have already seen.

When we set out to prove our presumptions, we scotch our chances of falling toward the miraculous. That's because being available to the mystery means being willing to believe that something more or different—something you literally cannot imagine—could be lying in wait for you. Indeed, when you surrender, you may step into an experience so huge and splendid and grand that, truly, you may feel as if you have stepped right out of this world. Yet miracles await us at every corner, in every dimension of our lives. We fall in love; our children are born; we stand on the street in a foreign city and meet the friend of a lifetime. Falling asleep, we dream, and in dreaming are given solutions to some of our knottiest problems. Whether in the unexpected and beautiful elevation of our daily lives as we ordinarily live them, or through the destined and magical introduction to a deeper life of the spirit, we are all being invited to come—to the larger world, the brighter light, the truer home.

Indeed, as we move through life we are continually presented with events and encounters which, in defying our expectations, quietly nudge us to change. The degree to which they can change us depends on whether—because of our minds we dismiss them, or whether, because of remaining beautifully open—we can receive what they are offering.

To be available to the mystery, therefore, is to be willing to be surprised—as a child discovers his face in the mirror, as a lover, undressing his dearly beloved, discovers the secrets of his adored. To be open to the miraculous is at last to be bountifully blessed. It is to move with grace, as you sweetly conduct your life, from the mountains of the mind to the rivers of the heart.

Know One Another Like the Seasons

The journey of love is a journey of many sweet knowings. It is the sweet bliss, in first love, of discovering all your love's little secrets, her favorite flower and fragrance, the color that sets her eyes off so, his plaid flannel shirt, the way he laces up his boots, his shaving brush, and that one wild hair in his eyebrow, the scent of her skin, the feel of her hair, the drawer she keeps her lingerie in.

It is, later, the being together of love—the sound of the key as he locks up the house, of the rain in the shower each morning, as, singing, she washes her hair. It is how she rolls over at night in the bed, how he sleeps, like a saint, with his hands folded over his chest; it is what he can fix; what she can mend.

And the changing, this way and that way. Arguing. Bad words and anger. And love in the midst. Making love, holding hands. And the children, wanting, not being sure about wanting them; being scared, and so overjoyed, and seeing them sleeping and carried, at night, in his arms; how he is so tender, how she is so easy, so strong with them.

It is watching the years go. Come and go. Come and come. Go

and go. Autumn and spring and winter and summer. So slowly and endlessly beautifully folding, unfolding. And so quickly go. And how we have done every year, so many things. And so few. Each day, and the meals and the work and the talk. Each day a small town with a map, and the trip we have taken in it. And the walks and the light, and the changing of the light. And how we have traveled. And how we have given the gifts. At Christmas. On birthdays. And all the words. The cards. The things we have said. The things we have whispered. I love you. Good night. I adore you. You are the one.

And how time has passed. He has grown old. And the white in his hair, and the fine, thin lines of his life and the sun are remaking his eyes; and her eyes, softer now, but still blue, and the so many years and the fading, and how the flower she loved and the color, and, yes, her perfume are still all the same; and how he still sleeps like a saint with his hands folded over his chest, and how the remembering now and forgetting are all a single long song, and how we have melted, woven ourselves, befriended, ensouled one another; how here at the end we know one another so well, like the bird knows the air, like the snowdrift knows the snow; and how he had said long ago, until we know each other like the seasons; and now it is spring now it is summer now it is autumn now it is winter; and we know we know we know.

The Truth in Love

Love is Truth; Truth is Love

LIVE THE TRUTH

There is nothing purer than the truth. It stands inviolate on its own merit, searing through falsehood and equivocation, shining brilliant as the spiritual totem around which our whole lives are organized. The truth is indivisible, stunning, eternal, the alpha and the omega of our mortal human existence. Nothing less than the truth can ever equal it; and nothing less than truth can ever pass for it.

Living the truth is an occupation of the soul at every level and in every compartment of our being. To live the truth with oneself is itself a journey, a life's work of self-reflection and discovery. To live the truth with another is a journey of risk and compassion. It requires listening, being open. It includes the empathetic moment in which we surrender expressing our own urgent truths in order to be present with another during the unfolding of his—or hers. To live in the truth with many others, with the larger whole of strangers and friends, or of the world community, is a exercise of the spirit. It asks us to grow, to expand. At times it may ask that we set aside, or even see as inaccurate or wrong, what we once perceived as the truth in our limited individual contexts.

Truth is a journey toward itself. To live in truth is to be aware that as your context changes, so will your view of the truth and the range of the truth that your heart and soul can contain. Your truth may not be now what it once was or what it will be in the future; but it is your duty to live and speak your truth of the moment and to be willing to change it, should some larger truth be revealed.

In relationship, we begin with the small truths—what's true at the moment for us—and speak them, in love, to the persons we love. We start with our stories, our needs, our hopes, and our dreams, then move on, through the many and varied vicissitudes of our ever-unfolding personal selves, toward the Truth that embraces us all. For the ultimate truth is immense; it swallows up all other truths, our little, individual truths, the contradictions we all are living, and even the bigger truths of paradox and dogma, of principles and rules.

Begin your journey toward truth. Search for the truth inside you that is longing to be expressed, and find the words to speak it. See the truth that stands in your midst, that is carried, embodied, and spoken by all your strangers and friends. Live the higher truth as you know it, as it is revealed to you—through art, in music, in literature, in nature and in dreams. Receive the truth that surrounds you, for the truth is everywhere. Surrender yourself to the truth, for truth is the ultimate light. Align yourself with the truth, for to live your life in the truth is to live in perfect freedom.

SEE YOUR BELOVED AS A SPIRITUAL BEING

We all know that there's more to a person than meets the eye, that we fall in love with the depth of a person, not just his or her surface attributes, and that there's something inside each person that calls us irresistibly, quietly to it. This is the spirit inside, the whisper of the divine that each of us contains.

It is connection with this essence that we seek in love, and falling in love is the moment when we are able to feel this divine whisper and see our beloved's spirit most clearly. In that sublime moment, we see in some way that's not quite magical yet not quite ordinary either, that this particular human being is rare, beautiful, and fine in a way that goes far beyond all the specific things that we might say about him or her. In this moment we have in a sense relaxed our ordinary perception and seen "through the eyes of love."

The eyes of love are, in fact, the open-hearted perceptions through which we are able to see not just the traits of personality, but also the shining of the soul. With such vision we apprehend not just the surface things—what he's wearing, how much money she has—but, for a moment, our beloved's divinity.

To continue to see your beloved as a divine being means that long after the rush and glow of that first perception have been dulled by the interference of the multitude of obligations and undertakings of your mutual life, you will still be able to turn, through the inner eyes of your soul, to the deeper truth of his being. You will see your beloved as radiant; as an infinite, beautiful soul; you will see her as the love she embodies; as the infinite joy that has found its home in him.

Unfortunately, as time goes on, we forget to practice this vision. Ordinary life takes over and we give ourselves over to it. Through the algebra of necessity, we replace the x of the divine in our perceptions, with the ABCs of emotions and the demands of everyday life.

But you can train yourself to remember. If you hold your heart open just a little bit wider, then love will become your lens. A million problems will instantly vanish and the scratchy difficulties of life as you normally live it will suddenly dissolve. By shifting your focus, you can look squarely, purely, into the eyes of the soul of this divine human being again.

There will be no differences then, between you and her, between you and him. Your differences will all melt in the radiant sameness you are. And you will be left, in the light of your soul, with your mirror of the divine.

Have the Courage to Say No

We are defined in life and in love not only by what we have the fortitude to undertake but also by what we have the courage to resist. In the long-ago movie, *Days of Wine and Roses*, a man and woman descended into a wildly gyrating spiral of alcoholism, all the while egging each other on. Finally, the man said *No* to himself, then even to his wife.

Life doesn't always ask us for such intense denunciations, nor is the path to our *noes* always so excruciatingly painful. But we all have things that we have to say *No* to—for ourselves and in our relationships—or else move in a direction that isn't for our highest good.

Sometimes these *noes* are small and simple, an unadorned statement of preference that's a quiet affirmation of your right to be yourself: "No, I don't want to go to the late show; I'll be too tired for work in the morning." "No, I don't want dessert." "No, I don't want to go to the party." Sometimes they ask for more strength, require that you actually take a stand: "No, I don't want to buy a . . .; we're already too much in debt," or sometimes, as in the unforgettable movie, they involve issues of life and death: "No, I won't give up my AA meeting just because you'd like me at home on Tuesday night."

Having the courage to say *No* means that you trust yourself and your relationship. It means you believe that your bond has the strength and resilience to absorb your *No*, as well as the power, as a consequence, to grow—in well-being, in moral fortitude. In saying *No*, you exercise the faith that the two of you, together, can live by the values represented by your *No*; recognizing that these values will take you to a level higher than the one embodied by the things that you are choosing to resist.

Sure, we could have five more drinks and lose consciousness. Yes, we could tell a lie and lose our integrity. Yes, I could capitulate to all your preferences and then resent you because I did.

A *No* is a choice for the good, the true, and the beautiful thing, and, in relationship, for the power, the beauty, and the possibilities of the relationship itself. Have the courage to say NO!

EXPRESS YOUR DEEP FEARS

Most of us are so emotionally crumpled and bruised that, when we're in love, we try to pretend that we're not emotionally crumpled and bruised. It's as if we feel so fortunate to have transcended our fears for a moment by falling in love, that we want to pretend to ourselves (first of all) and our beloved (as time goes on) that no emotional potholes exist on the back roads of *our* personalities.

It's a sort of misguided attempt at kindness to the person we love. I don't want him or her to know that I have a terrible fear of abandonment, a history of depression, a problem with money, an eating disorder, or that I live in the fear that my problem will someday overtake me. I love her so much; I want to give her my best, not burden her with my fears.

The thing about our deep fears, though, is that they always run the show. They're always in charge. They're always stronger and more powerful than anything we do to quell or compensate for them. They come from such a deep place in our psyches that, one way or another, they will out.

If your greatest fear is of being abandoned, and you don't share this as part of yourself to be healed, you will unconsciously re-create its enactment—just because you expect it so much. If your sweetheart doesn't abandon you right off, you'll act out something (become an alcoholic, a workaholic, or have an affair, for example) that will make him or her feel so rejected that he or she *will* abandon you, exactly as you "expected."

The same goes for all your other deep fears: of not being worthy, of not being smart enough or beautiful enough, of being controlled, abused, or overwhelmed. If you don't talk about your struggles, you're setting up the very situation in which they'll have to surface again, because our fears, like sad, abandoned children, keep knocking on the doors of our hearts until we let them come in.

So if you don't share them, open them up to be looked at and loved, they will diabolically run your life. Expressing them—openly, directly, tremblingly—creates deep intimacy. Fears dissolve in the pure light of day; they are washed away in the bath of true love.

ACKNOWLEDGE YOUR
RELATIONSHIP AMBIVALENCE

 Whether we know it or not, we are all living out our relationships according to some deeply embedded myths. According to these myths, whatever union we've formed—a marriage, long-term living-together arrangement, or the (at the moment) "romance of our dreams"—will be a totally satisfying, daily, domestic, exclusive, life-spanning affair.

These myths don't provide much breathing room. We're all trying to get to this blissful, perfect, contented state, but at times we feel boxed in. That's because no matter how well-matched we are, how deeply we love or consciously we cast our lot with another human being, we're all being asked to live in relationships that affirm our need for relationship but deny our need for freedom. We all have both of these needs. We need the security of connection, the bliss of bondedness, while at the same time we need the expansiveness of freedom—time spent alone to be our individual selves, the excitement and inspiration of our own unique collection of friends, opportunity to explore. That's why, no matter how much in love you are, how happy your are with your relationship, or how much you intend it to last forever, you probably still have a certain amount of itchy ambivalence about it.

This ambivalence, vaguely acknowledged (in the form of "nights out with the boys") or utterly suppressed (in the "you're my everything" songs), lies at the core of every relationship, and, at points of stress (when the longing for freedom and personal development win out over the desire for connection and belonging), can become the reason for "breaking up."

This ambivalence is so pervasive and unacknowledged because we can't talk about it. We think that if we "really" love the other person, we're not "supposed" to feel it. Thus we can't say, "I liked it when you were gone for six weeks; now that you're home, I'm feeling hemmed in—would you mind playing poker one night a week?" We don't say, "I love you madly, but for a week I'd like to sleep alone."

It's our inability to talk about the fact that, even though we do love, we also retain the need for private, individual experience that often presses us to express these needs as a final, desperate assault on what's an otherwise smoothly running relationship.

Although we can never entirely solve this quivering human paradox, we can approach a place of real peace if to ourselves and those we love we can at least begin to admit that having a relationship is a balancing act on the tightrope of this ambivalence.

ACCEPT WHAT IS

We usually mosey into relationships seeing their obvious possibilities, imagining specified outcomes, cocooning them with our own particular expectations. But what actually occurs is often shockingly different from what we expected. The person you wanted to marry has a phobia about commitment. The woman you knew would make a great mother decides to go off to law school. The suitor with the bottomless trust fund decides to give away all his money and live in a cave. Surprising revisions can happen on even the simplest levels: "When I fell in love with him, he was wearing a blue cashmere blazer and gray flannel slacks; but after I married him, all he would wear was sweatshirts and blue jeans."

Expectations come in two forms: general and specific. General expectations have to do with our dreams and plans for a specific relationship—that it will lead to marriage, that it will bring you children, that it will make you "happy." Specific expectations have to do with what we think we can count on day-to-day—he'll take out the trash, she'll handle the kids in a way I approve of. On one level, these expectations are all quite reasonable; it's appropriate to have long-range plans and goals and it's legitimate to expect specific kinds of participation from your partner.

But when your relationship becomes a litany of failed expectations—what you hoped for but didn't get—it's time to look at what's happening from an entirely different perspective. Perhaps, instead of needing to "communicate better" or "negotiate your differences" on an emotional level, you're being asked, on a spiritual level, to learn to accept what is.

Accepting—finding a way to be comfortable with things as they are—is actually a very developed spiritual state. It means that you've relinquished the preconceptions of your ego and surrendered to what's been given to you. Maybe he's not the provider you hoped for, but his spiritual strength is a constant inspiration; perhaps she's not the housekeeper you wanted, but the way she nurtures your children is absolutely beautiful.

Acceptance allows your spirit to grow. When you're able to recognize the little miracles and great lessons that replaced your expectations, you suddenly discover that what you hoped for was pitifully puny compared to what was actually in store for you and that, in a way far more complex and elegant than you yourself could have imagined, your life is following a sacred design.

So if you want a life that is larger than life and a relationship that is finer than even your wildest hopes, peel back your expectations and start to accept what is.

FACE YOUR DENIALS

Denial—actively forgetting, not admitting, not letting yourself know, see, face, or recognize a difficult truth about yourself—is a psychological position that most of us employ to one degree or another. Denial serves emotional and even spiritual functions. Denial is always a wall around pain. Denial protects us from the pain, abuse, abandonment, bad examples, and failures of love that are always hard to face head-on. But denial is a half-baked, temporary solution; and its consequences in the long run can be far worse than facing the pain that created it in the first place.

Consistently practiced, denial represents a spiritual compromise, a disability that threatens to limit our growth on every level. It cordons off attributes and behaviors in ourselves, which, so long as we hold them in denial, have the capacity to constrict if not utterly destroy our lives. Thus, the alcoholic in denial runs the risk of crashing her car, going to jail, losing her husband, job, children, social status, soul, and life so long as she persists in her denial; and the person who refuses to face his addictive use of credit cards runs similar risks.

Because of its very nature—an unconscious but deeply intentioned not-knowing—it's hard to see your own denials. Doing so requires courage and the expansiveness of spirit that will allow you to face your own negative aspects. If your present lover, an ex-girlfriend, five friends, six strangers, and a few enemies suggest that you have a problem with alcohol, that you're a passive-aggressive manipulator, that the way you handle anger is really off the charts, you'd better summon the courage to take a hard look (with professional help if you need it) at the truth that might lie behind these (admittedly hard to hear) accusations.

It's painful looking behind the curtain of our own denials. There's so much to face—old wounds, the fear that you won't have the strength to go on. Indeed, facing your denials takes courage precisely because it can feel more like an assault on your fragile ego and flimsy self-esteem than a step toward self-improvement.

But these hurdles are part of the process. Ego, and even self-esteem, if we hold them up too high or get too attached to them, can be strongholds of denial in themselves. We get so involved in protecting them, as image, that we forget the real person behind them. The truth is that there's nothing so fine as yourself—*you*, just as you are, with the feelings you've often been too scared to feel, with the flaws that are charmingly yours, with the sadness and hurt you *can* bear.

So take courage and face your denials, for behind your denials hides a radiant spirit, a whole, new, conscious self just waiting to face the truth, to finally be born.

RESPECT THE OPPOSITE SEX

It is certainly sad and seems almost strange that we must actually encourage or instruct ourselves to respect the opposite sex. Yet unfortunately, because for decades we have been so bombarded with attitudes, articles, and books that underline the differences between men and women, we now live in a world where we are surrounded by antagonism between the sexes. For the sake of union—in society and in our intimate relationships—we really must consciously choose now to honor the opposite sex.

Honoring means remembering the value of, cherishing, holding dear, celebrating rather than disparaging the differences between, remembering the beauty of, enjoying all the contrasts, savoring in clarity the blessings of the other. It means not building walls out of differences, but delighting in each beautiful amusing one, as the counterpart and balance to our own splendid gender's hilarious uniqueness.

It also means moving from the surface to the depths, realizing that beneath the familiar costumes of gender we all embody a similar evolving consciousness, that inside we all carry as great emotional treasure the same exquisite array of feelings. A man's grief over the death of his father is no less real than a woman's grief over the loss of her mother. A man's heart will be as poignantly, beautifully touched by a breathtaking sunset, the rustle of cottonwood leaves in Yosemite, or a cool, crystalline autumn morning as a woman's. At the core we are all moved by our sorrows and by the magnificence and miracles that touch us, not as men or women, but as human beings.

To know this is to relax the wearying focus on our differences, to come graciously into the knowing that we can honor one another without harming or shortchanging ourselves. It is to remember that what we live and suffer, we live and suffer in common, and that real love, love in the soul, is beyond male and female, beyond gender as an issue at all.

Be Open to Receive the Message

Life is awash with messages for us. They come in many forms, arrive in unexpected packages, ride in on a wide variety of frequencies. If we *hear* the news that there's going to be a hurricane, we're likely to change our plans; if we *see* a movie and are moved to tears, our hearts begin to open; if we fall down the steps, running out the door to catch the commuter train, we're being "told" to slow down. And if you should recognize the love of your life at a workshop, decide to sell your house and move to Paris to be with him, you're being shown that life can be magic. All these are messages; and if we're open to receive them, they can utterly transform our lives.

Most of us think that we receive information through our eyes, ears, noses, and hands, and of course we do; but as well as allowing information in, these organs of perception also serve to *limit* our perceptions. When we listen with our ears, we may *hear* sound but not apprehend the full meaning of what has been said. When we *see* with our eyes, we may observe an object but not necessarily apprehend the essence that lies within it; and when we *touch* with our hands, we may not have felt all there is to feel.

Being open to receive the message—whatever its form—means being open with your consciousness. It means that instead of settling for your mind's translation of the messages your sensory organs have received, you will also be available with your body and your heart to hear, see, feel, and know.

The body has a knowing and the heart a wisdom far beyond the seeing of the eyes, the listening of the ears, the sensing touch of our hands, and even the sniffing of our smart noses.

Indeed, listening with your body is a supremely receptive experience, for the body is a totally sensing instrument. Through it, messages can be apprehended directly—as a chill, as a pain around the heart, a quickening of the pulse, a blurring of the vision. In the body you can suddenly "know," beyond a shadow of a doubt, the thing which before you could not apprehend. The same is true when you listen with your heart. The heart has no categories, no little boxes, no way of saying good or bad, yes or no. The open heart is a well of reception; it is moved in its entirety by what it has perceived.

It is our sacred opportunity in this life to expand and expand until we can become receptive to every message, no matter its timing, whatever its form, to be open to such a degree that we can apprehend the truth embodied in everything and everyone. To do so is not just to be well informed; it is to have a larger, more conscious life in every dimension.

Practice the Courage of Criticism

Criticism, the words through which you straightforwardly evaluate and report on another's behavior, including its negative aspects, is one of the most courageous undertakings of any intimate relationship. It requires responsibility, generosity of spirit, integrity, and thoughtfulness to offer the kind of criticism that can be a portal of transformation for the person you love. (Timing, of course, is important too, for there are good times and bad times to criticize.)

We often think of criticism as purely negative, the harsh cutting down of a person or his behavior, until his spirit is broken. But it doesn't have to be that way; in fact, legitimate criticism is really an art form. Well done it can be a fine tool for the shaping of character and personality, a compliment of the highest order. It says, in effect, I see that you're a person of value; I trust that you want to improve, and in my heart I'm holding the image of who you could be at your finest. Criticism, graciously offered, becomes, then, a form of encouragement, the vehicle for another's refinement.

Most of us don't know how to criticize well—to acknowledge what's already good about someone before rushing off to nagging and judgment. It takes love, integrity, and insight to honor the person you're correcting while at the same time offering legitimate, negative reflections. To criticize well requires that you accurately identify and then carefully express exactly the flaw, mistake, or style of behavior you believe could improve with change.

Here's how to do it: (1) Identify precisely the thing that you feel moved to criticize, for example, that you always leave the lid off my calligraphy pen when you borrow it. (2) Evaluate whether the thing you're criticizing is just your personal preference or whether it's actually something the person could benefit from changing. ("I like blue napkins; why did you buy pink?" versus "When you leave the lid off my pen, the ink dries out and in the future we might not be able to use it.") (3) Consciously and carefully state your criticism in a way that honors the person but still points out the behavior he or she could benefit from changing: "I notice you left the lid off my pen. I wish you wouldn't do that. The ink dries out and then it doesn't write properly; I get irritated when I find it that way. Besides, you write so beautifully, it would be a shame not to have a pen that works the next time you'd like to use it." (4) Check to see if the person has been able to receive your criticism and if any part of it has been misunderstood or was too difficult to hear, go over it again with different words until you get an affirmation that it has been received.

Offered with integrity, your criticism can be a great gift.

Open Your Heart to the Life-Changing Remark

Receiving criticism well is an act of self-esteem and courage, a highly developed stance requiring trust, resilience, discrimination, and willingness to change. You couldn't possibly let criticism in if you didn't believe that you have value in the first place—or that you're strong enough to withstand the remarks that are being levied at you without being reduced to shreds.

Receiving criticism requires trust, because in doing so we surrender our own consciousness to the perceptions, consciousness, and good will of another. We say, in effect, I'm willing to consider that what you're saying about me at this particular moment is even more real than what I, in general, believe about myself. You're also saying you trust that your beloved truly has your well-being at heart, that you believe what you're going to be told is something that will allow you to grow and isn't just an attempt to wipe you off the face of the earth.

It requires resilience because you have to, in fact, be sturdy and flexible enough emotionally to take in these ego-redesigning comments and put them to good use—make the change, alter the behavior, rearrange the attitude—and know that you as yourself will still be there after you've implemented all the suggested revisions.

And, finally, you have to have discrimination, because not every criticism *is* legitimate. Some criticisms pinch because they're to the point; others are so far off that we're offended to even have to listen to them.

Here are some tips: (1) Stay open-minded. Listen; take in before you react. Remember, this may be something of value. (2) If the criticism fits, take it all the way in and make the changes it invites. (3) If you're not sure it fits, mull it over, keep the part that belongs, and toss out the rest; and if it's really off the mark, say, "Thank you kindly, but this doesn't feel like it applies." (4) Say "thank you" no matter what. Appropriate criticism can smooth out your path, and, true or untrue, criticism always provides an opportunity for self-examination.

Delivering criticism is an art form; being able to receive it is an act of trust, and being willing to exchange it with your darling is a landmark on the road of conscious love.

Integrate the Divine Erotic

Your erotic life, the expression of your sensuality in every dimension, is the mysteriously lovely vehicle for the integration of all that you are as a personality and a spirit. It is the sacred playground of physical passion, the point in our experience more than any other at which the material and spiritual intersect. Here the physical body becomes a temple of joy, of deeply rooted connection, of solace, of coming home.

Through sensuality, emotions are expressed in physical form. The body knows, feels, and teaches, eloquently and directly. When we are touched in exactly the right way, when making love is graceful and ecstatic, we are moved without words to a level of integration of body, mind, and spirit that can be instantly healing.

Because of the power of sexuality to heal the rift between our bodies and our souls, we all have a yearning toward it that is far stronger than what we can attribute to the physical sex drive alone. That is because deep inside we know that the erotic life can lead us to integration. And it is only people who are healed physically, emotionally, *and* sexually from the great raft of wounds we have all endured (if in no other form than our culture's repression and perverted exaggeration of the erotic) who can be true vessels of compassion and approach the whole world with generosity.

Unfortunately, many of us have been unable to welcome our bodies, our innate sensuality, our sexuality, and the power of the erotic itself into the ken of the spiritual. We're not even sure that we should, and yet like our sense of the spirit inside us, we do somehow vaguely understand that our erotic life, too, is divine.

If sexual energy and the joy it creates weren't so awesome a power, no one would bother with it. Instead of being so focused on it, in so many forms, good and awful, we would have gone off to live quite comfortably without it. The truth is that sexuality is a light of such incredible brilliance that it draws the moths of darkness to it; and for this reason, if for no other, it is a spiritual responsibility that we integrate the divine and erotic in our lives.

In your grand quest for love, therefore, for the finest and most beautifully integrated becoming that your heart can entertain, do not overlook—indeed consciously seek—the sexual healing that will bring your personality and spirit into alignment with your body. For when we integrate our sexuality, claim it as the amazing gift it is, we not only heal ourselves and our partners, we help to restore the divine erotic to the entire world.

Recognize the Longings of Your Spirit

We are spirits, visitors, explorers here on earth, who have stepped into life in human costume. We are here because we choose to be, because we wouldn't have missed it for the world, because life is a gift—and so very beautiful.

But as spirits we're also a little bit sad, ambivalent about the obligations of this life and of the material world. That's because the spirit is free. It has no substance or contents, no projects or objects. Its essence is pure essence; its purpose is pure being. When spirit engages with matter and we become human beings, our soul still holds a memory of what it was to live in freedom, before the confines of embodiment, intellect, and personality restricted our timeless, radiant essence.

Thus it is that as human beings we always carry deep within us the longing for a nameless something, a way, a place, and a grace of living that seem endlessly to elude us. Like a dream whose images vanish just before waking, like the passion whose most exquisite moments cannot be kept and crystallized, like the sound of distant music, faintly entering a room, we ever so evanescently remember the life of pure spirit we lived before we were born.

It is this remembering that makes us at times feel sad about being merely human. We love the beautiful things of this world, but they never quite fill our spirits. Our bodies are magnificent: they bring us the great joys of passion, but they fall away like a husk at the end; we know that they are not *us*, that we are not them. We fill our lives with the familiar human undertakings—careers, achievements, professions— and our clever, ingenious creations—works of art, music of every sort and order, dancing—and our spirits are moved . . . remembering . . . yet not quite made ecstatic by what we have said and done.

This niggling but ongoing dissatisfaction we constantly feel with life, no matter how fine and grand it may seem or how beautifully we may have constructed it, is the sign of our true essence. For we are of spirit. And spirit is boundless, a breath in the vast white wind of the infinite soul. Our discontent is its whisper, calling us back to the real beyond real, reminding us where we came from, enticing us back home.

Tell Your Beloved Your Story

 Especially if we've been connected for a long time, we think we know each other. We do, of course, know a whole array of things about one another, but it's really only when we tell our stories—the touching vignettes that embody our struggles, sweet moments, disappointments, or wild hopes and dreams—that our most real, most vulnerable selves are revealed. Indeed, if we don't tell each other our stories, we're all one-dimensional, blank screens on which we project our assumptions about one another.

Everybody has a story, and because we all do, when we hear each other's stories, we feel suddenly connected. Story is the great river that runs through the human landscape, and our individual stories are the little creeks that flow through us all to join the river at its source. When you tell your story, however, you open yourself to the level of fragility which, as human beings, we all share; for, no matter how different our stories, at the bottom of them all is the well of pain from which we have each dipped a draught.

Tell your darling your story—the most painful event of your childhood, the most exciting moment, the greatest regret of your adult life—and you will discover, in depth, a self you never knew. That's because, between the sentences of our stories, the gist of things slips out, not merely the facts, but the feelings that have shaped us, the point, in anyone's journey, from which there was no return.

For example, although you may be aware of your husband's fascination with architecture, you may not understand why he never pursued it, until you hear the story about the night his father got so angry at him for staying up late drawing that he broke all his drafting pencils, threw them the trash, and raved, "Since you're wasting your time like that, you're never going to get a cent to go to college." Or, you may know about your wife's interest in astronomy but not know where it came from, until you hear the story about how when she was a little girl and heard her parents downstairs arguing at night, she would lie in her bed looking up at the stars until—she could swear—the stars beamed their white light right into her room so she could finally go to sleep.

When you tell your personal tale, spinning and spinning, telling, retelling, the tight thread with which you have wrapped up your pain will gradually start loosening. And when you listen to your beloved's story, he or she will become, in the process of your listening, a fully formed human being. So tell each other your stories. They're more than entertainment for the dinner table or a long ride in the car. They are your selves, spelled out and spoken, brought forth in time and in your own language, a loving gift you give to each other.

Be Conscious of Your Unconscious

Consciousness, being aware and being aware of your awareness, is a gift of the human condition. It is in consciousness, the state of being awake, that we act, we choose, we behave. We do what we are "conscious" of, draw from choices we actually recognize, behave in ways we realize we are behaving, and see that the outcomes we intended materialize into being.

But fluttering beneath consciousness lies the murky sub-basement of the unconscious. Here the memories, experiences, and events that have shaped our lives lie deep within us as the hidden motivations that are quietly directing our behavior all the time.

We all have a great many things stored in our unconscious—hurts of childhood so exquisitely cruel that we can't consciously remember them, a multitude of little stinging events that affected us deeply—but we really don't know quite how. Because often we haven't dredged these things up for conscious examination, and healing, we can, with unconscious carelessness, hurt ourselves and others with them.

When a hurt or fear from childhood is randomly stimulated ("he rearranged the furniture three times, and I was scared that, just like my father, he'd never be satisfied with anything"), we may instantly attack ("I can't believe you spent all day redoing the living room. You're insane!") or do any number of other hateful things.

Unconscious behaviors have an uncanny power to direct—and undermine—our lives. Whether or not we know by name all the mad dogs roaming around our unconscious, it's our duty to be aware (on the conscious level) that there *is* a pack of mad dogs down there. We are responsible to ourselves—and to those we love—for our unconscious as well as our conscious behaviors. Unconsciousness is no excuse; in fact, in relationship, it is the supreme irresponsibility.

Little slights of the unconscious are the normal mistakes of not being able to empathize fully or of letting out small bits of anger in little unconscious acts—"I forgot"; "I didn't mean to"— but big deeds of the unconscious amount to interpersonal crimes, and we are responsible—and fully culpable—for them. In this realm exist the vast array of acts that run the gamut from the wife who flirts at a party because she's angry at her husband for being so late coming home, to the father who beats his son to a pulp because earlier that day his boss lambasted him.

We all have things that can turn us into monsters, and some of our unconscious acts can ruin our relationships, (to say nothing of our lives.) Therefore it behooves you to discover your deep secret motivations, for in relationship (and in life) we are absolutely accountable for committing such personal "unconscious" crimes.

Seek the Common Ground

 In the tit-for-tat world of our psychological dramas, we tend to make life adversarial. We take sides. We look at intentions and effects—she was late just so I'd feel bad; he said that just to hurt me. We seek redress for our insults and wounds; we keep score (you were late more often than I was, you bounced more checks than I did, you hurt me more than I hurt you, you're meaner than I am, well, anyway, you were meaner more times than I was).

It's as if in trying to find peace in our relationships, we think keeping score will win the day. If I treat you like an enemy, show you all your crimes, and *prove* that you're guilty, you'll decide to make up for it by loving me more because you feel so bad about how gruesomely rotten you've been.

Unfortunately (and fortunately), a lover or sweetheart isn't like a corporation that can be sued (and required to make recompense) for a faulty product. We don't "pay up" in love because we're shamed or proven guilty. In fact, the stronger inclination is to get away from the heat and head for the hills. Taking an adversarial position will only make an adversary of your mate; and adversaries make war, not love.

That's why, when conflict arises, we need to look for the common ground. In the midst of the fray, when we seek the kernel of truth that can bridge us to understanding, we can find our way back to union.

We all have a dark side; we've all hurt one another more than we'd like to admit. But even our misdeeds merit an attempt at understanding, because the truth is that even dastardly acts are born of pain. That doesn't excuse them, of course, but it's important to remember that even the difficult, hard, hurtful things we do to each other spring from the woundedness within us. When I can comprehend your suffering (and, therefore, the crooked behavior you perpetrated on me) and you can comprehend my pain (and therefore my wrongdoing to you), we can stand face-to-face in compassion, unravel the missteps we've made, and together start over from a different place.

So if in your heart of hearts, you seek union, pleasure, companionship, support, and nourishment from your beloved, don't make an adversary out of him or her. Even in the hairiest fray, try curiosity and kindness—"*Why* were you late?" "Why *were* you so short with me?"—and you may find out something surprising (I got back a frightening mammogram today. The guy right next to me in the gym keeled over dead."), something which, instead of turning your beloved into the enemy, will fill your heart with compassion.

Hold Your Beloved
in Special Awareness

When you love someone, at a soul level, you carry a very special awareness on behalf of that person. In the deepest abyss of your being, you have agreed to know, see, sense, and feel for your beloved with a subtle kind of attention that constantly takes the truth of his or her being into account.

The attention we carry for one another in this way runs the gamut from holding a quiet place in your heart so your beloved can go through his emotional healing, to knowing that the person you love needs money, time, or space, even when she isn't consciously aware of it and can't ask you for it directly. Sometimes our refined perception takes the form of "just happening by" at the moment of crisis. At others, it may mean holding the awareness that the person you love has issues about her health, weight, body image, or a particular physical feature, and acting sensitive and supportive around that particular issue. You may hold your beloved's truth in awareness by recognizing that the person you love has a deep fear of abandonment to which you respond by being realistically reassuring, generous, and steadfast in your expressions of love, or by knowing that your sweetheart has been sexually abused and consciously encouraging him to discover his boundaries or seek her own emotional healing.

Sometimes we carry this awareness consciously; at other times our awareness is secret even to us, a brilliant act of intuition that just seems to occur. The man who brings home flowers "for no reason" only to discover that minutes ago his wife received news of her mother's sudden death has unconsciously "sensed" her pain and met her need before she could even express it. Similarly, the woman who "doesn't know why" but shows up at her husband's office with lunch only to find out that earlier that morning his biggest deal of the year fell apart, is also acting on an intuition unconscious even to herself.

This sort of intuitive second-guessing is a gift of love. It means that, rather than expecting your beloved to know, recognize, understand, and consciously verbalize every single thing that he or she needs, you will step in at times, recognizing the unspoken, and address it with your own intuitive kindness and care.

Is this codependence? Not if it's offered in consciousness (rather than out of dependence or low self-esteem); not if it's given in full awareness, as a conscious act of love—and not if you can accept it when it's given to you in return.

Raise the Consciousness of Your Love

Trying to help the one you love to a lifestyle, level of consciousness, degree of freedom, success, or creativity that, to you, seems like nothing more than the obvious fulfillment of who that person really is can feel like an endless task at times, especially when he or she hasn't so much as acknowledged the gift you've been so consistently giving.

Perhaps you've felt your husband's need for a new job and have plopped down thousands of want ads on his desk, only to discover that he's ignored them all. Or you've tried to nurture your wife's self-esteem by complimenting her on her beauty and buying her carloads of fine lingerie, but she's still fretting about her fat thighs and fine hair. It's frustrating, isn't it?

Precisely because it's invisible, the gift of awareness (and the things we do because of it) often goes unacknowledged. If your partner knew he needed these things, he could consciously ask you for them, but since he doesn't, he can't; and, in fact, it's his very lack of awareness that developed *your* awareness in the first place. As a result, we often feel hurt, used, or abused because of what we have given. If that's how you're feeling now, here's an exercise so you can go on giving your gift without plummeting into a pit of resentment. (Here, I'm using the example of a woman who is helping her husband with issues of incest; you'll want to modify the process for yourself.)

Sit with a lighted candle between you, and say the words that apply. For example, "At the level of my soul, I am holding a deep awareness for you and helping you in various ways because of it. I need you to become conscious of this now and to thank me for what I am doing so I can continue to love and serve you in this way.

"In loving you, I am carrying the burden of your battered self-esteem because of your childhood incest experience. In love I am offering to assist you in healing that wound by refusing, along with you, to be in the presence of the person who abused you, supporting you in your healing process by helping to pay for your therapy, being willing to listen to you and receive your anger about your abuse when you feel the need to express it.

"I ask you to now acknowledge that I am carrying this burden for you, to tell me that you need me to, and to thank me for so doing."

Your partner should respond by saying something like: "I acknowledge that you are helping me recover from my sexual abuse. Thank you for meeting my need and for serving me in this sacred, beautiful way. I ask you to continue until my healing is complete."

When you have finished, you can then exchange roles, for we are all, always, carrying a burden of awareness for each other.

Seek Your Emotional Healing

Emotional healing is the radical transforming of your emotional wounds that results in the revivification of your body, the nourishment of your mind, and, ultimately, the illumination of your soul. In a sense, life itself is a healing journey through which we are moving from a state of forgetfulness about the true nature of our divine being and into a state of remembering and total illumination. It is because our emotions are the arena in which we can so often get derailed in this process that it is of such great importance that we seek our emotional healing. Since, in Western culture, we've been taught so much to perceive ourselves as emotional beings, we tend to stay focused on our emotional vicissitudes, and so long as we have unresolved conflicts on the emotional level, they will stand in the way of our moving on to the higher levels of love.

Sometimes we seem to be operating on the principle that everybody else was born perfect, and it's only a cruel quirk of fate that, unlike everyone else (who's still perfect), we've got some ugly knots to untie. Not so. What is true is that within the basic perfection of the gift of life, we're all given certain difficulties, limitations, and problems as a kind of meditative theme to unravel throughout our lives.

Whatever we must heal—immobilizing fear, explosive rages, abandonment in one or a hundred forms—is grist for transformation, opportunity for enlightenment. For, each time we encounter one of these devastating limitations, we are invited to move through it and, once having healed it, to connect with a higher level of consciousness. On your journey, for example, you may be asked to expand your emotional repertoire from passivity to rage, from rage to forgiveness, from forgiveness to compassion, and from compassion to indivisible love.

Because love is our ultimate destination, this journey of healing is your life's true work. It doesn't matter whether you undertake it with additional help from psychotherapy, meditation, tai chi, weight lifting, Alcoholics Anonymous, the Baptist Church, vegetarianism, or an intimate relationship. Any path to healing, devotedly pursued, can deliver you to this destination—for there is no other. What does make a difference is whether or not you take the journey. If you don't, you will live awash in self-pity, endlessly tossed by your feelings, your unfinished emotional business. But if you do, you will see that what started out as your painful limitations became in the end your most radiant assets; and your soul, released at last from its endless emotional involvements, will emerge as the shining envoy of your love.

ALLOW YOUR NEEDS TO BE YOUR GUIDE

If you would allow yourself to be guided by your needs, your needs could become the path that would lead you to yourself—*and* also to your beloved. Conversely, denying your needs or endlessly serving others to the detriment of fulfilling your needs, are both ways of not discovering who you are and of not allowing yourself to be loved.

Not needing is an inauthentic state, a denial of your humanness, because one of our truest, most basic characteristics is that we are creatures of need. To deny this—by being brutally self-sufficient, by manipulating others into serving you, or by pretending to have transcended need—is a form of spiritual hypocrisy. No one alive on the planet—not even avatars and saints—has totally transcended need. Indeed, to be human is to need; and to need is to be human.

We need food. We need loving arms. We need air and light and the sun and the glistening fine white shine of the moon. We need to be listened to, magically; with velvet ears, to be heard. We need empathy, to be feelingly felt with. We need work that is a true expression of our spirits. We need company, compatriots on the path. We need witness: mirrors, friends, and strangers to reflect to us who we are.

We need success—at something. We need peace.

Our needs are like weeds that spring up between the rocks on our path—insistent, organic, demanding. They are our barest, boldest truth, the essential grit at our core. But often we don't treat them as such. We tamp them down and shut them up and talk ourselves out of them right and left, for so long that, often, by the time someone's ready to meet them in relationship, we don't even know what they are.

The opposite of not knowing your needs is becoming conscious of them—discovering what they might be and then finding the words to express them. As their size and shape and content (and the deprivations and losses, frailties and talents to which they refer) are all gradually revealed, you will gain a map of yourself. You will see who you are, what you really do need, and what joy it would bring to your heart to have your needs fulfilled.

So discover what you need, speak up about it, and be open to receive. For to know what you need and to ask for it—clearly, strongly, directly—is an act of personal strength. It will allow you to be honored through the meeting of your needs, and it will allow the person who loves you the joy of loving you well.

Inhabit the Paradox of Urgency and Surrender

The path of the heart is paradoxical. It moves, always, simultaneously, toward both urgency and surrender. When we fall in love, our hearts feel desperate and excited. We are driven, exhilarated, longing moment by moment to be in the presence of our beloved. We count minutes, days, and hours, indulge in outrageous extravagances—diamonds, perfumes, airplane tickets—all in the name of love. At the very same time, we're in a state of surrender, having given our whole selves over to the love that has overtaken us. We'll do anything, go anywhere, say good-bye to everyone else, all for the sake of love, because our heart has been opened and filled. For the moment, our heart's occupation is the art and practice of love.

As a relationship continues, so, too, does this pattern of urgency and surrender. Day by day, and over time, we desire certain outcomes—intimacy in communication, social compatibility, conscious partnership, sexual bliss. In a different way now, the heart is driven by longings. In this process, it engages effort—what about that couples' weekend, those tantra workshops, or even twenty minutes a day for an intimate conversation.

But at the same time the heart is involved in these projects, we are also being instructed by the soul to accept that the heart's intentions may not all be fulfilled. We are asked to surrender to the fact that the results in any arena—our conversations, our level of economic comfort or sexual intimacy—may not be of the quality we had originally hoped for. Indeed, we realize that we may be obstructed at almost any corner and that now the emotional task has become to surrender to what is.

Urgency is that which ignites us, sets our hearts on a path, molds our relationships in a conscious, intended direction. The fuel of urgency is emotion—wanting, seeking, desiring, holding a life-changing vision. Surrender, its opposite, is letting go of desire and intention, floating free in the sea of events and experiences that is continuously changing.

Spiritual maturity in love is the capacity to inhabit this paradox, to live at once in the state of both urgency and surrender, to both "work at" and "give in to" love. This is true as we fall in love, in the midst of our intimate relationships, and on the path of life itself.

As you surrender to the paradox, you will gradually find serenity. Stop trying to figure everything out; and let the paradox embrace you with its controversial arms. You will find yourself wrapped up in a billowing sweet peace—the peace of living at once in both urgency and surrender.

FACE YOUR DIFFICULTIES HEAD-ON

 Even in every successful and agreeable union, there are differences (some irreconcilable) and incompatibilities (some vast) which are the mysterious irresolvables upon which that relationship becomes a kind of meditation.

Most of the time, we live with these difficulties as a kind of wearying background noise to the interplay of our relationships. They haunt us as sorrows, frustrate us as unmet needs, prickle our consciousness as irritating secrets and unexpressed resentments. How we handle—or don't handle—them has a great effect on our relationships. Keeping the difficulties to yourself (whether they be imperfections of your partner or of the relationship itself) won't make you feel any better, nor will it move you toward bridging the distance that your differences represent.

What does hold the possibility of creating change is facing your differences head-on and lovingly talking about them—Facing and Telling, as I call it. What this means is that you will dive into even that most risky of emotional waters—sharing with your partner the things that are irritating or disruptive.

This involves, first of all, being truthful with yourself about what these things are: It *really is* totally unacceptable to me that, he's started smoking again. It scares me; I feel like he's killing himself. . . . I wish she had a spiritual life—it's painful to me that we can't pray together.

Once you've faced the truth by yourself, hold on to it. Don't blurt it out; instead, write it down on a list. Then, with your partner, pick a time to talk about these things. You might want to do this regularly, once a week or once a month, just to keep the emotional slate clean or, if you prefer, choose a single, specific time when your secret "grudges" have mounted up.

The format, then, is to say very simply: "I need to tell you what's difficult for me right now"; then state, without anger or judgment, what's bothering you at the moment.

Your partner, the listener, should then respond by saying, "Thank you for telling me this; I'm sorry this is so difficult. I hope that in time, together, we can move beyond this problem."

In this ceremony, each partner takes a turn, both in revealing what's difficult and in responding. This isn't an exercise in making promises to change behavior. *It is simply about revealing and acknowledging the difficulties*, accepting that they exist, and believing that your relationship is strong enough to contain the truth of what you both reveal. When you've finished, conclude the process with a kiss and say "I love you" to each other.

Move to the Spiritual Level

 We all come to terrible impasses in our relationships—fights we have over and over again, stubborn character flaws that just won't budge, irritating habits that can almost drive us crazy. When we sit in the midst of these things, we can feel angry, bitter, and stuck. In our minds we recite the ways we've been wronged, how terrible he or she's been, how hopeless our relationship is.

The truth is that we've all been wronged; and seemingly unbearable things do happen. There are issues in our relationships that we do go round and round on, and no matter how much we "work on," negotiate, talk about, or attempt to solve them, we don't seem to make much progress.

At such times, we can feel really discouraged or we can look at our relationships through a different lens. Instead of seeing them as existing to satisfy our every whim, we can lift them up to the spiritual level and ask ourselves what it is that we're being invited to learn. If you thought of the problem as a lesson, what would it have to teach you? If you thought of it as a divinely ordained detour, what might it be saving you from? If you construed it to be an invitation to grow in some new direction, what would that be? By lifting it up to the spiritual level, you can begin to see everything that occurs in your relationship as an opportunity for spiritual growth.

That's because whatever is happening in a relationship is happening simultaneously on the emotional and the spiritual levels. When you view it only on the psychological level, you can keep going around and around in a rat's nest of unresolved problems. But when you lift it up to the spiritual level, let it ascend to where the bright light of truth can shine in, you will, I assure you, see something quite different. There, instead of focusing on the nuisance of the moment as this week's edition of the hopeless situation, you will see that every event in your relationship is something that showed up to expand, inform, or refine you. Instead of endlessly blaming yourself—or your beloved—for the difficulties that inevitably transpire, you will see them as serving a higher purpose—the development of your soul.

When we move to the spiritual level, we recognize lessons, instead of blaming for errors and mistakes. We see our partners no longer as those who fail to fulfill all our hopes and dreams, but rather as those whose spiritual task it has been to embody the very frustrations through which (by struggling and chafing against them) we develop spiritual maturity. This also eases us on the emotional level, for when we can feel compassion instead of judgment—for ourselves and our beloved—our relationships become instantly sweeter, deeper, and more gracious.

Protect Your Soul

The journey of the soul is not all joy, nor is it always consummated in the light, for in this life there is a choosing at every moment of what our soul's destination shall be. Just as in a dance one may move in any direction—forward and sideways, fly beautifully elevated or be bowed down toward the earth—so in life do we also, constantly, through every infinitesimal increment of our behavior choose a direction, the path our souls will take.

If a man kills his wife and uses the legal system's loopholes to escape conviction, he has not only gotten away with murder, he has lost his soul. He may be set free, return to the usual circumstances of his life, but he will never *be* free; he will be a soulless man whose very existence is the embodiment of untruth. No matter how many people he may falsely convince of his innocence, in the light of the truth he is still condemned; and should he try insanely to convince himself of his own innocence, then surely his soul shall be lifted by darkness from him.

There is no neutral moment or action in our experience. Everything we do, every action we enact, every nuance of movement, each word we utter either creates the further illumination of our souls, or moves us in a direction in which, in a moment of dark unconsciousness, our souls can be utterly compromised.

The potential for loss of soul—to one degree or another—is the affliction of a society that as a collective has lost its sense of the holy, of a culture that values everything else above the spiritual. We live in such a spiritually impoverished culture—and in such a time. Loss of soul, to one degree or another, is a constant teasing possibility. We are invited at every corner to hedge on the truth, indulge ourselves, act as if our words and actions have no ultimate consequence, make an absolute of the material world, and treat the spiritual world as if it were some kind of frothy, angelic fantasy. In such a world the soul struggles for survival; in such a world a man can lose his own soul and have the whole culture support him, and in such a world, conversely, the light of a single, great soul that lives in integrity can truly illumine the world.

The Beauty of Love

Beauty and Truth are the Joy of Love;
Joy and Truth are the Beauty of Love

PURSUE BEAUTY

Beauty is luminous radiance. Beauty is lucent, mystical essence, the face that is unforgettably lovely, the dance with the exquisite movements that our minds cannot erase, the music whose notes repeat themselves endlessly in our hearts. Beauty infuses; beauty enthralls; beauty inspires and illumines; beauty lifts up and enlivens our souls.

Beauty applies to both the material and the ethereal worlds. Beauty calls on our organs of perception (she's a beautiful woman) as well as our spiritual sensitivity (it was a beautiful experience) and mystically coordinates these worlds for us. Whereas beauty is embodied in form, the apprehension of beauty, whatever its form, is an experience of transcendence. It is this remarkable capacity of beauty to be at once both immanent and transcendent that causes us to pursue it, to be moved by it, and to recognize that in some ineffable way we can trust it as the measure of what has value for our souls.

Beauty also enchants us because its essence is to embody *more*, a higher level of whatever it is that we are perceiving. In standing above all others, the beautiful thing invites everything around it to rise to its own level. So it is that the beautiful moment teases us to make all moments beautiful, the beauty of the written word to elevate our own language, the sound of beautiful music to surrender to the beautiful soundless stillness in our own hearts.

When we have soul-filling experiences in nature, when we lose ourselves in the ecstasy of orgasm, at times of searing joy, when the veil is lifted and we glimpse the sacred frame of life, we are experiencing beauty, a taste of our true eternal state of being.

We often step into a relationship for some quality of beauty it contains—she was beautiful; he was playing beautiful music when you first walked into his rooms; he has a beautiful heart; she has beautiful hands—and it is this same quality, beauty, that will elevate your relationship and cause it to ascend. Great beauty is both a gift to be received and a state to be pursued.

So fill your life with beauty. Allow your beauty to shimmer forth. Anoint your house with beautiful things: objects, fragrances, movements, moments, sounds, emotions. Beautiful food is a sanctification of the body. Beautiful ideas are a feast for the mind. Beautiful art and music are a banquet for soul. We must seek beauty, respond to it, cultivate it, and surround ourselves with it, for beauty in this life is a reflection of our souls, as our souls shall be forever a pure reflection of it.

Learn the Language of Intimacy

If we think of ourselves as protected by many layers of emotional cotton batting, then intimacy represents the gradual unwrapping of these layers until we stand in one another's presence with the secrets of our hearts unveiled. Intimacy is achieved through the communications that spring from our depths and reach to our depths. The more we partake of such communication, the greater the sense we have that we are not alone; that, in fact, at the core we're all deeply connected.

The communication of intimacy is an art form all its own. It has its own style and language. Unlike the conversations of business, which focus on facts and figures, or the language of pleasure, which often takes the form of planning—what movie to go to, where to get the best ice-cream soda—the communication of intimacy springs from emotion and uses a language which is, by definition, personal. It uses the word *I—I* need, *I* feel, *I'm* scared of, *I'm* having a difficult day; *I* love you so deeply—and it focuses on feelings.

Indeed the communications that create the deepest sense of intimacy are the clear, strong, beautiful words through which we bring out the feelings we have deep inside. When you express your feelings (as opposed to your opinions or ideas), you create a sense of intimacy because you're showing your real self.

You will find the exact words for your feelings when you just look inside yourself and ask, what am I feeling? What do I need to say right now? And then take the risk of simply and directly putting it into words. Whatever you feel—your secret hopes, your feelings of shame or inadequacy, your fears, your hurt—deserves to be expressed. When you express these things out loud, you open a window to the sensitive inner corridors of your being and invite your beloved to shine a light in.

Until we dare to speak from this place, we will be condemned to the superficial in relationships—who's going to pick up the kids, why the oven doesn't work. We will never feel close, known, or connected so long as we play it safe in how we communicate. Indeed, the language of intimacy *is* the language of risk. It takes chances by putting you, your consciousness, your personality, and your emotions—the great ones and the lousy, ugly, icky ones—all on center stage.

So if you truly want intimate communication, an experience of emotional and spiritual closeness, start speaking your feelings—and realize that reaching this point of connectedness won't just come out of nowhere. It will take work (practice) and grace (really speaking the heart-touching words) and risk (the willingness to reveal yourself)—but it will certainly be worth the effort.

Be Patient, Gentle, and Kind

Patience is a quiet virtue, the ability to willingly wait for what is unseen to be gradually made manifest. Patience is faith, the conviction that what you imagine, need, or believe to be the highest fulfillment of how you think things ought to be—for yourself, for your relationship, for the whole amazing span of your life—will gradually and beautifully reveal itself in time. Patience with one another is also a quietness of spirit, a deep inner knowing that rests secure that you are on the right journey, that your beloved is with you, and that no matter the pitfalls or detours, you can stand at his side, be in her presence, quietly waiting . . . with patience.

Gentleness is the soft virtue, the cloudy featheriness of spirit that allows you to move toward the person you love, and through each circumstance you face, in an easy, graceful, and gracious manner—touching delicately, listening openly, feeling with empathy, seeing with eyes of compassion. Gentleness eases the way, adds refinement and grace to the journey, softens the blows, cushions the sorrows, lightens the burdens.

Gentleness can be everywhere: in what we say, in how we move, in the people and circumstances we quietly choose to bless ourselves with. It is moving easily instead of roughshod through life; speaking with kindness rather than blurting things out; leaving time instead of blusteringly rushing through things; making room for the stranger who arrives, the beautiful thing that unexpectedly happens.

Kindness is the sweet virtue. It soothes and calms and renews. It remembers, adds touches of color—blankets and bed socks and flowers. It offers the unasked-for word, the spirit-cleansing compliment, the nurturing embrace. It is soft; it reaches out to mend and amend: *Can I help you? Is there anything I can do? I'm sorry. I hope things will change.* Kindness is the unnecessary necessity, the unasked-for moment of beauty that adds a hopeful texture to every measure of our lives.

Love waxes and wanes with the seasons, with our hormones, and our circumstances, but love of the heart and soul must be constantly nourished and tended. Patience give us hope for the future; gentleness gives us grace in the moment; kindness dissolves the wounds of the past. Be patient and gentle and kind, and the love you hold as a treasure now will beautifully flourish and last.

Value Your Precious Incarnation

Our bodies are the sacred chalice, the elegant Rosetta Stone computers in whose cells are stored the memories, dreams, and contemplations of our entire earthly lives. They are also the physical constructions of our lives, and it is through their very configuration and how we choose to live in them that we play out the themes of our lives, through growing, changing, and healing.

We often think of our bodies as somehow separate from ourselves, as if our minds were our true identity and our bodies a sort of pull-along toy that follows behind us. The truth is that our bodies are the very vehicle for our experience of being human. We know what we feel because our emotions are registered in our bodies; we remain in the human experience only so long as our bodies are still alive. Far from being extraneous, something apart from ourselves, our bodies are actually—and marvelously—exactly who we are.

For a whole variety of reasons, most of them involving pain, many of us are cut off from our bodies. Thus, as we inhabit them—doing our work, haphazardly or intently pursuing our personal and spiritual destinies—and as we share them in relationship—in nurturing acts of compassion and in making love—we are unable to receive the deep grounding they were meant to bring us.

For many of us, the body no longer "rings true" as the measure of anything. Thus we cannot sense danger, know truth, or feel love through our bodies. Rather than being the seat of absolute knowing, the inviolate guide for every dimension and action of our being, we experience them more likely as demanding, high-maintenance objects— *I ought to lose weight; I should start working out*—or spoiled children with minds of their own—*but I want to have dessert*—which, from time to time, we try to discipline.

We have done a beautiful job of educating our minds and encouraging ourselves in achievement—in all the things that support the notion of the body as a separate entity. But the true beginning of wisdom about ourselves resides in our bodies. For not only are our bodies not separate from us, they are the very habitation of our being, cell by cell interwoven with our personalities, and the container of the soul's capacity for love. For the love of our souls is *embodied*. It flows through our hearts and breathes in our bones; and to partake of life fully, we must start from and return to this inescapable knowing.

Look After Your Body

We often think of our bodies as our own private possession, and, of course, in a fundamental way, they are. But when you're in a relationship, your body is also the medium of your connection to your beloved. If you didn't have a body, you wouldn't be here to love anyone in the first place; and it is your body, your physical presence, with which the person you love is continually engaging. After all, it's your body you bring home from work every day; it's your body that sleeps with your darling at night. You have to look in the mirror to actually see how you look; but the person who loves you has to look at you all the time. When you're exhausted or depressed, your darling will see the weariness in your face, your stance, just as he or she will also recognize your sense of well-being, vitality, and happiness.

Because of this, the way you treat your body carries great significance in any relationship. It can be a gift, an asset, a joy, a grand celebration for your beloved, or a detriment, a burden, the occasion for a spiritual test. Just as radiant health and well-being can present beauty and inspiration to the person you love, so physical self-abuse or neglect can become the reason why your relationship starts to break down. If you don't take care of your body, you're sending a message both to yourself and your beloved—because how you take care of your body is a reflection not only of how you feel about yourself but also of how you expect your sweetheart to feel about you. If you're in the process of destroying your body in one way or another (by smoking, drinking to excess, being a workaholic, sugaraholic, caffeineaholic, or sit-down-at-the-desk-and-never-get-any-exerciseaholic), how can you reasonably expect your darling to delight in and enjoy your body or to reflect to you the love you haven't been able to give to yourself?

In sharing your body with the person you love, you are sharing your true essence. So honor that essence, the highest human expression of your embodied soul: by nourishing, loving, and cherishing your body—for yourself and for your beloved.

Practice the Art of Empathy

Feeling *with* and for someone—having empathy—is the deepest form of emotional participation that you can have with the person you love. In your intimate relationship it can make you feel more known and knowing, more fully recognized and seen, more beautifully, deeply connected.

Empathy is an emotional engagement. It is entering the Badlands of another person's emotions and camping out there with him, allowing yourself to feel what he feels, to be moved as she has been moved, to fear, grieve, and rage, as if you yourself had been touched, frightened, bereaved, or driven to anger.

Having empathy isn't necessarily easy. Indeed, of all the emotional interventions, empathy is the most demanding. For, to actually be able to enter into another person's experience so fully that she is able to *feel* your presence there with her is the embodiment of the highest degree of emotional refinement. To truly join your beloved—in the place of his powerlessness, or of her shame—is to have already, in some sense, visited these hellish realms on your own.

The supporting cradle of empathy is constructed from the huge array of feelings we have already felt in our own hearts and bodies. If you haven't first felt a particular feeling, or if you're unwilling to revisit it, your capacity to feel with another will be fuzzy, halfhearted, and dull. Your empathy will be a feeble attempt at sharing the feeling, but not a truly empathic experience.

That's why empathy is such hard work. You have to do your own work first, to acquaint yourself, in depth, with your own emotions. Only then will you have, as it were, an *Encyclopedia Britannica* of the human feelings to refer to; because you have felt, you will "know what it feels like." You'll have a reference in your own body, an idea in your own mind, of what a particular experience is likely to feel to another person. Since you've "been there," you can truly empathize.

Unfortunately, one of our inhibitions in the practice of empathy is that we're often afraid of revisiting our own emotions when someone else is in need. Instead of being able to step into another person's experience, we're so afraid of being overwhelmed by the conscious recollection of our own painful feelings that instead of offering empathy, we deny ("It's not so bad"), problem solve ("Here's what to do"), or minimize ("You think that's bad? Let me tell you about what happened to me.").

To be capable of empathy, therefore, become the master of your own emotions, not in the sense of control, but in the sense of allowing your feelings to flow through you. Then you'll be able to give that most precious of all emotional gifts—the gift of empathy.

LIGHTEN UP

Life is miserable, boring, serious, and awful enough that you don't have to be so uptight, logical, organized, responsible, and on time all the time. Lighten up!

Yeah, but what about . . . the dwindling dollar, the falling Dow Jones average, your dog's license, your driver's license, the registration for your car, income tax, the rent, dental problems, medical problems, law suits, marriage counseling, your aging parents and their problems, your teen-age children and their problems, the two million problems leftover from your childhood that you still haven't solved, not to mention where the clean shirts are, where your car keys are, and what about that ugly stain on the rug. . . .

You will never run out of things that have to be handled in this life. And they will never give you joy. There will always be a few more clothes to pick up at the cleaners; the checkbook will always need to be balanced. Before, during, or after doing any of these things, you will not feel particularly happy—they won't light up your life.

What will light up your life are the sweet things, the beautiful small things that bring stinging half-tears to the edges of your eyes. What lifts your heart in the moment? What are the beautiful things you remember from two hours ago? *(Such a touching conversation with a stranger, her voice like the broken thin feather of a bird. I could feel her courage. She cried a little, talking about a song she wanted to write. It would be about ordinary things, she said, . . . like love.)*

Or yesterday? *(The way the light was, orange edging the blue in the late afternoon and how in the light you could feel the coolness of the air, how for a moment temperature and color were the same.)*

Or the past five years? *(How he loves me and what a surprise it is that he does. . . . I had never imagined. . . .)*

They are not responsibilities, any of these things that brushingly beautifully touch your soul, that make you feel dancy, that sparkle your heart. They are silly and priceless and foolish and free. Lighten up!

NOURISH YOUR HEART AND SOUL

When we identify too strongly with the material world, we can lose track of our precious hearts and souls. We can almost begin to believe that it's the things of that world—objects and possessions—that will bring us happiness. The truth is that it isn't things, but experiences—the moments and feelings that move us most deeply—that truly connect us to our real selves. Discovering what these things are is a process in itself, and partaking of them with your beloved is one of the deep joys of relationship.

To nourish your heart and soul, you must first comprehend that your heart and soul require great nourishment. Once you have understood this, you must make time and room for the things, experiences, and people who feed you deeply in these realms.

Nourishment of the heart is sweet personal love, the endless sensitive play and interplay of all the emotions that exquisitely fill us and charm us, the sense that we are desired, that we have been chosen above all others to be loved, that we are one of a kind, irreplaceable, precious, and rare. This love of the heart is also awakened by romance, sweet gifts, sensitive words and affectionate touches, beautiful evenings and sweet afternoons, elegant moments, fabulous passion.

The food of the soul is more rare. Our souls are nourished through mystery, through the experience of beauty, through witnessing and partaking of things and experiences which, in themselves, carry a reference to the eternal—great music, color, the fragrance of roses, mountains; the meadows, trees, and rivers that long ago held great meaning for us. Although these things have always been here to partake of, it is the way in which we experience them in elevated moments that allows them to speak to our souls of the unseen world, the unheard sound, the bliss we cannot yet feel but can only vaguely imagine. When we slip through the sieve of our ordinary lives and fall into the bottomless depths that these experiences open to us—we pierce, if only for a moment, the illusion that life as we know it is all there is.

For each of us there are such things. Some appear unasked for as gifts—others we must consciously pursue; but no matter how they come to us, when we are fed in this way, we instantly sense that we have been truly nourished. The famished heart can give no love; the starving soul can neither imagine nor remember its own sacredness. Indeed we cannot love truly until our own hearts and souls have been filled.

So put yourself in the presence of the things that nourish your heart, that can beautifully feed your soul. Drink deep on your own and also with your beloved. Separately and together, nourish your hearts and souls.

CONSIDER YOUR BELOVED

In an intimate relationship, no man or woman is an island. Everything you do—your words, your actions, your habits, your conscious and even your unconscious behavior—affects your beloved. When you drop a stone into the pool of your union, the rippling circles reach a long distance.

That's why it's important, always, to consider the person you love. Consideration is emotional generosity, a way of gathering your beloved into the reality of your experience in such a way that he or she feels both included and looked after. This means that as you fashion your plans—I'd like to move to Tulsa, there's a great job opportunity there; I'm going to get up at 5 a.m. and go running; the next time your mother comes over, I'm going to let her have it—you realize that whatever you're cooking up will also have consequences for your partner. Will she hate Oklahoma? Will he wake up and not be able to get back to sleep if you get up at the crack of dawn to go running? Will his fragile truce with his mother be shot to hell if you really do tell her what you think of her?

Considering your beloved means that you realize he or she may have a point of view or circumstances that will be affected by the decisions you are making. It doesn't mean that you give up your own needs, forgo your plans, or, like a mindless wonder, so thoroughly consider your darling's desires that you abdicate your own (He'd be uncomfortable at the party, so I won't go.) It just means that, at all times, you'll remember that the person you love is also part of the equation.

Considering your beloved means, in the first place, keeping in mind that everyone else has their own reality too. You are not the king or queen of the world; what's good for you is not necessarily good for everyone else. It also means that after (or, better yet, right when) you're going through your own changes or making your own plans, you consult your beloved for his or her reaction: "Do you think you could get used to Tulsa?" "If I get up early to run, do you think you'll still be able to sleep?" "It's hard on you, too, isn't it, that I have such a difficult time with your mother?"

Consideration is a very delicate form of love. It's a quiet feeling you carry in your heart. Unlike the grand gestures of love—the Hope diamond, the four dozen red roses—or even the magnificent sacrifices of love—she donated one of her kidneys to her husband—consideration is the quiet stream of conscious caring that bonds us to one another, the promise that at all times and in every way, you will carry a sense of your beloved's well-being under the sheltering wings of your love.

CUDDLE UP

The trouble with life is that it's not cozy enough. In the baby-part of ourselves, which every one of us still has, we all need to be hugged and cuddled, deliciously, sweetly curled up with and kissed, to be lovingly tenderly held.

Cuddling is nurturing of the body and the spirit and we all profoundly need it. To be touched and held, to have our skin—that miraculous fine thin silken wrapper of our being—caressed, addressed, remembered, and cherished, is one of the greatest human requirements. It's a leftover need from childhood, when most of us didn't get cuddled enough, didn't get held, or kissed, or lovingly touched, or dearly nestled nearly enough. We wanted to lie up cozy, safe, and sweet near our mother's heart, to be tossed in the air in our father's strong arms, but it didn't happen quite often enough. We didn't get to sit on quite enough laps, didn't get our backs scratched, our tummies rubbed, our feet tickled, our curls brushed, or the backs of our necks kissed nearly enough.

That's why, now, we need to cuddle up, why we long to feel the gigantic embrace that grown-up cuddling is. We want to feel protected and safe. We want to feel nurtured and loved. We want to feel that there's more to life than just our chores and our work. We want to believe that having a body in a world full of bodies isn't a sad, lonely joke. We need to be cuddled so much, in fact, that if we're not, our hearts cry out—with tears, with overeating and alcohol, with the overwatching of television, with anxiety and depression. The truth is that we're all—every one of us—touch-starved human beings.

Cuddling, therefore, being cozily with—on the couch, in the bed, on the sidewalk, in the kitchen, in the car and at the beach, in elevators and airplanes, in restaurants and subways, during the credits at the movies and in long lines at the bank—is an unadulterated pleasure that fills a giant human need.

Cuddling isn't a stand-in for any other thing—like sex, or a great conversation, or a night out on the town, or a trip to the lake, or your favorite baseball game. Cuddling is wonderful, helpful, healing, delicious, delightful, soothing, yummy, cuddly, and scrumptious all by itself. So cuddle up!

Pay Attention to Timing

Timing is the mystical component of any relationship that refers to *when* things happen. It's the perfect moment, the magical conjunction of events, the folding together of one person's movement through time, with another's—in perfect harmony.

Relationships themselves and every event, behavior, and action within them have their own unique and perfect timing. Just as the ideal mate often shows up only when you've completely given up on ever falling in love, so it is that within the sacred walls of a relationship there are perfect moments for everything, a choreography of timing that can either support or detract from the grace of your relationship.

Timing is a sensitive reflection of myriad things about us: our histories ("I can't stand to do the dishes right after dinner because my mother was so compulsive she'd start washing the dishes before we even finished dessert"), our metabolisms ("I'm just not a morning person"), our methods of apprehending reality ("I'll never get it if you talk about it for an hour; tell me what you need, let me go for a walk, and I'll be able to give you an answer when I get back"), our emotional sensitivities ("I just can't handle more than one complaint at a time; my father used to sit me down on Saturday night and read me a list of all my mistakes for the week"), and our just plain personal quirks ("I don't know why—I just wake up at 4 a.m.").

Sensitivity to timing is awareness of the propitious moment, span of time, or appropriate circumstance for any given happening. It is the intuitive awareness that there is such a thing as the perfect moment—to say the word, to initiate the sexual encounter, to offer the gift, to express a complaint. Being sensitive to timing in relationship means that you will be conscious, first of all, of your own needs about the appropriation of time—for privacy, for being together, for handling conflict, for making love, for doing your share of the chores. It means also that you will communicate your needs and preferences and be aware that your partner's rhythms may be entirely different from yours. Timing, just like who pays what share of the bills, is something you must negotiate.

Sensitivity about timing adds grace to any union. If, together, you don't cultivate this sensitivity, you'll be continually jamming up against the differences in your time frames, saying the emotionally loaded thing at an inauspicious moment, or generally feeling abused in the realm of time. Conversely, when you learn to choose the perfect moment—to say the heart-touching words, to present the sapphire ring—you'll turn your relationship into a beautifully choreographed performance of the exquisite dance of your love.

Rediscover the Harmony

Harmony is the spiritual beauty of any intimate relationship. It is elegant coexistence, peaceful compatibility, a similarity of frequency. It's knowing that you share the same view of the world, that what you want out of life runs along parallel lines. It's looking at your beloved and being able to say to yourself: "We stand for the same things, don't we? We may encounter some rough spots, but at heart we both share the same values."

In relationship, harmony is a gift of the spirit. It is a mystic similarity of essence that allows you to operate—both separately and together—from the comfortable wellspring of knowing that between you there is a sacred resonance. In a sense, it's the very reason you chose each other in the first place—if there weren't a certain degree of harmony between you, you wouldn't have thrown your lot in together and established a relationship.

When there's harmony, you can feel it; it will add grace to all your undertakings—your work, the rearing of your children, the way you conduct the actions of your daily life, the way you handle conflict, and what you perceive to be the underlying deep direction of your life.

Unfortunately, life scratches and claws at the harmony of our relationships. Too many demands in too many forms can undermine the pleasant ground of any union's harmoniousness. Schedules, children, unexpected little assaults from others, can all make us feel at times as if there's no harmony left between us.

Conversely, harmony is nurtured and restored by being lovingly remembered. So if the harmony is out of balance in your relationship, ask yourselves the following questions:

After all the fuss and fray, when the kids are in bed, when the fight is over, is the stream of our life together most of the time so good, so flowing, that, in general, I can give thanks for his or her presence in my life? In what ways are we, at the core, a complement, a mirror, a balance for each other? What things still give us pleasure together? What is the higher purpose of our relationship and what is our common undertaking?

If you have a hard time finding answers to these questions, take a good look at what's compromising the harmony in your relationship. Is it something you can change? Is it circumstantial—your wife's been on the road for a month—or is it an emotional issue that needs to be dealt with? What is the one thing you could do or say right now that would be a first step toward restoring harmony?

Harmony is the spiritual balance in any good relationship. So give thanks for the harmony you have, develop the harmony that's missing, and nurture the harmony that ensues.

Honor Yourself

As souls, when we come into life, we step out of the timeless eternal and into the finite moment of living as human beings. In this moment, and in the remarkable context of living on earth, we become both agents and receivers of the gifts of personality—that vast, amusing, unique, and frustrating array of attributes and attitudes, predilections and possibilities, from which we compose the symphonies of our individual lives. No human being is exactly like any other; and no matter how much you may share with, be influenced by, or bond with another, only *you* can be yourself.

It's a pleasure and a privilege to be yourself. Just being born is a compliment. Having a chance at life, to feel, see, and live it, in precisely the way that *you* will, is a sterling, never-to-come-again opportunity.

It's easy to forget this. We sit in our lives, sometimes feeling stranded, hemmed-in, and alone, not liking who we are, not being happy to be here, disparaging our precious selves. But being a self, living out your uniqueness, is precisely the beauty of being alive, and when you ignore or forget to celebrate your uniqueness, you insult, in effect, the consciousness that gave you life.

If you, who live, breathe, suffer, and enact all that is yours uniquely to experience, are unable to value all that you are, who can? And who will? Honoring you is *your* job. Nobody else can do it. Nobody else has the knowledge or experience. And nobody else should have to, for self-honoring is your first work, the ground of loving recognition from which your talent for honoring others will inevitably spring. To honor yourself is to know yourself, in a truly valuing way; and no love you have or share or give will reach its full dimension until and unless you have first learned to truly honor yourself.

Honoring yourself means seeing *you*, recognizing *you*, loving and cherishing *you*. It means that of all the human beings on the face of earth, you celebrate yourself: your depth; your sensitivity; your wisdom, whatever it may be; your talents, whatever arena they fall in; the mysterious, beautiful path of your own particular history; your inner beauty; your body; your emotional, physical, spiritual strengths; your wit, your humor, your intelligence—all that you have been, all you are now, all that, in time, you will be.

So honor yourself. From this conscious loving acceptance of all that you are will spring all the love you can offer to others. Honor yourself!

LET GO OF IT ALL

When in doubt, let go—give way; give in. When in expectation, frustration, or pain; when in confusion, impatience, or fear; when you don't know what to do next; when you're losing control—let go. Let go. Let Go. LET GO.

Letting go is emotional and spiritual surrender. It means willingly jumping out of the lifeboats of your preconceptions of reality and taking your chances out in the open sea of anything-can-happen. It means that even as your definition of reality is dissolving before your very eyes, you willingly relinquish it, instinctively comprehending that the state of surrender itself will be a creative condition.

It's hard to let go, to live in the formless, destinationless place. All our lives we're taught to hold on, to be the masters of our fate, the captains of our soul. Letting go isn't comfortable; it can feel like anything from laziness to utter loss of control. It's not aggressive and self-assured. It's not the American way.

But letting go is, in truth, a most elegant kind of daring. It is vulnerability of the highest order, an emptying out of the self, of all the clutter and chatter that, ordinarily, we all contain—ideas, attitudes, schemes, and plans—and offering your self as an empty vessel to be filled. In this emptiness there is room for so much; in this vacancy, anything can happen: breathtaking transformations, changes of direction, miracles that will purely astound you, love that comes out of the woodwork, spiritual conversion. . . . But only if you are willing to truly let go of it all: as the tree dropping her bright leaves for winter, the trapeze artist, suspended in midair between the two bars, the diver free-falling from the high-dive—have all unequivocally, wholeheartedly let go.

Letting go is being alive to the power of the nothingness. It is living in surrender, trust, and the belief that emptiness is at once the perfect completion and the perfect beginning. So let go. And remember that should you hang on to even a shred, or try to make a deal with the gods ("I'll let go, but only if . . .") then nothing new—or wonderful—can happen.

Offer Loving Service

Most of the time we think of love in terms of what love can do for us, imagining that when we "fall in love," all our dreams will come true. We want so badly to have our own feelings recognized, our own needs met, our own insecurities handled, and our own desires fulfilled that the notion of love as service is almost inconceivable to us.

We can get so caught up (or bogged down) in the notion of love as a what-will-*I*-get-out-of-it experience that the idea of serving another is extremely distasteful. At a deeper level, we're afraid that by serving we might lose the sense of our selves that we've worked so hard to attain. But in its purest state, love is service, a wholehearted offering so satisfying that it doesn't feel like service at all, but rather self-fulfillment of the highest order.

Most of us still need practice for this particular outreach of love. We're not sure how to serve or what our true service might be, and we haven't practiced serving to such a degree that it feels second nature, graceful, or effortless to us. The truth is that we're all already serving in one form or another. If you're a parent, you're serving your children. If you've cared for an invalid neighbor or an aging parent, you have also served in love. If you've bandaged the wing of a wounded bird, given a homeless person a dollar, saved a stranger from drowning, given up your seat on the subway, then you too have served in love. These are the seedlings of service, the places in which our hearts have started to open, but should you choose to have your service grow into a huge and sheltering tree, you will be given many opportunities to mature your gift of true service.

Begin by asking yourself the following questions: What does it mean to serve? What would *my* true service be? How can I develop my service so it can truly become a gift of love?

Service in love is temporarily setting aside your own needs, wants, and priorities and allowing the needs of another human being to become so radiant, so vivid, and so pertinent that, for a moment, your own are dissolved. This gracious moment *is* love, and the more we live in the practice of service, the more we create this love. For when we serve one another, we also serve the great cause of Love.

SEEK THE DELIVERANCE POINT

The deliverance point is that exquisite moment in any personal encounter or life experience in which we arrive at a state of resolution about what has troubled, violated, or detained us; and we stand free to move to the next level of our unfolding.

Getting to the deliverance point isn't easy. We want to be magically lifted up out of the conflict, whatever it is: the horrible, repetitive, seemingly insoluble argument; the hateful job; the gnawing feeling of insecurity; a particular chronic irritation (his tardiness, her raucous laughter); the vague feeling of alienation that, in general, we are quietly subjected to by living in such a fast-changing world. We want to reach the deliverance point, but often don't want to pay the price—going *through* instead of *around* whatever the problem is.

To arrive at the place of the "Aha! I've made it out of the pit of hell," we need to be willing to crawl on emotional all-fours to get to the destination. This means, in relationship, being willing to have the fight (whether you're scared of your anger or not); to initiate the discussion (whether or not you feel foolish); to say what you need (whether or not he'll be able to give you what you've asked for); or to negotiate (even though you've never been able to agree on this particular issue before).

It's when you've gone through it all—said the thing that was so hard to say, made the decision that seemed impossible to make, fought the fight you thought could put your whole relationship in jeopardy, expressed the needs you were sure would never be filled—that you can finally bring yourself to the deliverance point. Mystically, amazingly, sometimes after you've given up even believing that such a place could exist, you reach a resolution that seemed impossible only moments before.

Getting there takes courage and practice and will. But it's worth it. Start now by telling yourself that there *is* such a place—it's a real destination—and then do whatever it takes, no matter what hurdles you have to jump or walls you have walk through, until, victorious, relieved, transformed, you arrive . . . at the deliverance point.

CELEBRATE THE "WE" OF YOU

It is because in the "we" of union that the individual 'I' becomes ever more beautifully defined that we enter into relationships in the first place. Somewhere, intuitively, we all know that love will make more of us than we ever would have become on our own. So without so much as a breathtaking pause, we "fall in love," give ourselves over to the charms of our beloved, and surrender ourselves to the mysteries of union.

Here everything changes. Through each nuance of behavior, whether a kiss, a conversation, the income tax, or making love, you are asked to take account not only of your beloved, but also of your relationship. That's because when you fall in love, there's another spiritual entity—the "we," the "us"—that is brought into being. Although it's invisible, it is utterly alive—vibrant, vivid, and unique; continuously present as a discrete though subtle energetic essence. You can feel it when you're alone together as the mysterious unified play of your two energies. You can recognize it when you present yourselves to the world as the wave of response you create as arm-in-arm you enter a room. It's the constellation of ideas and points of view which, as a pair, you embody, the joy which, as a couple, you bring to all those around you. It is neither the sum of you both nor a negation of either of you. It is the mystical interaction by which an additional identity is created, where one plus one equals three, not two.

It is this entity—relationship, the embodiment of opposites attracting, then uniting; strangers gathered at the same hearth; lovers, together, under the stars, bidding good-night to the day—that we are acknowledging when we speak of ourselves as a "couple," "Mr. and Mrs.," "my sweetheart and I," "we," or "us." "*We* had a wonderful time at the party." "It meant so much to *us* to go to Germany." And this entity, like the individuals in it, must also be nourished.

When you honor your relationship—by speaking adoringly of it to others, by treating your sexual relationship as a sacred bond, by standing fast together in times of turmoil and sorrow—you strengthen the power of your union. You nourish the "we" as the precious being it is, celebrate the unique, unrepeatable identity it has, and reweave the blanket of love that will warm and protect your union always.

CONSECRATE THE MATERIAL

Life on earth is both cluttered and graced by objects. We live in a material world which has at once the ability to illuminate us or to drag us endlessly downward toward the mundane. The material world is not what we ordinarily consider to be the habitation of the sacred. In fact, in some schools of thought it is held to be the very antithesis of the life of the spirit. At times in our own lives, in order to make some forward movement in our spiritual development, we may need to divest ourselves of material things, get rid of possessions, and seek the lack of encumbrance that our spirits require to grow.

To make the material sacred, however, is to utilize it in such a way that, rather than detracting from the life of the spirit, it stands in eloquent support of it. To do this in a world that has mishandled its material blessings is a highly developed spiritual undertaking. It asks us to see that everything—even possessions and objects—can be consecrated to love.

Early in our relationships, we intuitively know the sacred meaning of objects. The gifts we bring are shining tokens of love; the wedding rings we exchange, the material symbols of sacred commitment. But all too often, as time goes on, possessions become an end in themselves. We want things. They're important to us. And rather than being instruments that serve in the cause of love, objects and their acquisition can become the focus of a relationship.

It's not that we don't need possessions, don't need our houses, cars, and stereos. But a home, no matter how humble, can also become a place that truly nurtures your spirit. Indeed, you can decorate your house, choose a given piece of furniture or of art, or select a sound system and music to create the physical environment that will support—rather than take the place of—your deeply felt love.

Instead of wanting and having more and more things, ask yourself what things you have and which you might acquire that will really give you joy; what objects create a feeling of serenity for you, of inspiration, of happiness? Will it please you to see a vase of flowers on the table (whether it's Baccarat crystal or a clear glass tumbler from Woolworth's) or would you prefer the serenity of emptiness?

Your environment is your sanctuary. Allow it to be such. Not all of us can afford the expensive things that are so beautiful that, just in themselves, they confer a sense of loveliness to our environment. But we can all begin to hold our objects in a sacred way, to choose them with care, to insist that they serve us in spirit, and to ask that they stand as a reflection of the love that should be the highest focus of our lives.

BE GRACEFUL, HOPEFUL, AND WISE

Grace is beauty of the spirit. Hope is the optimism of the soul, and wisdom is the soul's intelligence. These all are qualities of such eloquence that even as we hear the words, a quiet settles in our beings, as if from a far distant place we have heard once again the names of the elegant ancient virtues: Grace. Hope. Wisdom.

Grace, hope, and wisdom are all qualities of the soul. They refer to how our spirits operate in the world; they call up a sense of our deeper engagement with reality, and tell us again that, over, around, and through everything, a beautiful spiritual consciousness is quietly operating. So it is that grace adds a quality of silkiness to all our movements, not only the way we move with our bodies, but the way our spirits inhabit them; not only the way we move through the world, but the way in which, because of our genteel openness, we allow the world to move through us. Grace is beauty, refinement of the spirit. We feel it, recognize it, are beautifully softened and engaged by it, whenever we stand in its presence. In bringing us into its comeliness, grace brings us into our depth. We hold it as the measure of what we may longingly aspire to as the spiritual grandeur in our lives.

Hope is promise. When the present seems unbearable, hope allows us to live in the future and there to find ease. When we hope, we partake of the state of absolute calm that has already understood that everything we have done and everything we shall do, will be beautiful somewhere, sometime; that our sorrows will enhance us, that even our tragedies will bring us to our depth.

In wisdom we know without learning; we apprehend without effort. We remember what we were never told and can offer it, graciously, easily, as the truth that heals, the observation that clarifies, the intuition that illumines and brilliantly transforms. Wisdom is the soul's intelligence delivered, shared—the soul's ancient knowledge unself-consciously revealed—in words that ring with the truth we have always known but never before been able to fully perceive.

Grace makes life fluid, flowing, and fine. Hope makes life lucky, exquisitely foreseen. And wisdom allows us to know when to trust grace and hope. Grace, wisdom, and hope are not shiny little virtues, but grand powers of the soul that will insist through their stunning magnificence that everything else in your life rise up to meet them. For when you cultivate grace, hope, and wisdom, they will require in every arena that you become much more than you are, that you step through your old limitations and envision a larger world, a world breathtakingly beautiful, alive with possibility, and abundant with the power to truly redeem itself.

LIVE IN THE LIGHT OF THE SPIRIT

With each person who passes through your life, you have a soul agreement. What this means is that long ago, in the realm of the soul, you promised to have some special encounter, share some life-shaping experience, complete some soul-honing work with that particular soul in this life.

Soul agreements are commitments to the evolution of our individual souls in conjunction with one another, as one by one we make the journey to that state of seamless awareness that the mystics call enlightenment. It is because of these agreements on a soul level that at times you may feel a mysterious strange connection with some other person, why difficult people may at times inexplicably inhabit your life, why you may find yourself on a journey with a particular person—as if you had an unwritten contract to fulfill—and then discover that, as if by amputation, your association is suddenly over.

As the community of souls who have gathered together in life on earth, we have agreed not only to remember for each other the pure state that was our origin, but also to act out whatever portion of the endlessly changing tableau of human experience we have been called upon to play to ensure our own soul's growth and that of the souls to whom we have made these deep promises. Some of us are here to be beautiful and strong, others to be cranky and difficult, some to die young and teach us through the searing heartbreak of great loss, others to live long and instruct us through wisdom. But no matter what role we are playing, we are all enacting a part in that one great spiritual destiny, which is to remember our eternal essence and move toward ultimate union.

So it is that every person you meet, each soul who crosses your path and affects you—wonderfully and terribly, briefly or for a lifetime—is here for that reason, and every relationship you engage in is but a small scene in the vast, ever-unfolding human panoply that is being endlessly enacted for the purpose of your soul's development. When you recognize this, you will suddenly, breathtakingly see that each person has been brought to you with a high and elegant purpose, that each soul has come to touch your soul and teach it, that each relationship exists to hasten your own soul's beautiful awakening. No longer is anyone a stranger; no longer can any of your relationships be seen as failures or mistakes.

In the light of the spirit, we see that we are all playing out roles that are the fulfillment of an exquisite and all-encompassing plan. To recognize this is to step out of conflict and into grace, for when we realize that life has been so beautifully designed, we will bask in the light of the spirit; we will live in absolute peace.

If you wish to read any other of
Daphne Rose Kingma's lovely books about love,

TRUE LOVE
How to Make Your Relationship
Deeper, Sweeter and More Passionate

A GARLAND OF LOVE
Daily Reflections on the
Magic and Meaning of Love

WEDDINGS FROM THE HEART
Ceremonies for an Unforgettable Wedding

you can ask for them at your local bookstore
or order them directly from **Conari Press**
by calling **1-800-685-9595**